Nick Vandome

OS X
Mavericks

Covers OS X version 10.9

In easy steps is an imprint of In Easy Steps Limited
16 Hamilton Terrace · Holly Walk · Leamington Spa
Warwickshire · United Kingdom · CV32 4LY
www.ineasysteps.com

Notice of Liability
Every effort has been made to ensure that this book contains accurate
and current information. However, In Easy Steps Limited and the
author shall not be liable for any loss or damage suffered by readers
as a result of any information contained herein.

Trademarks
OS X® is a registered trademark of Apple Computer, Inc. All other
trademarks are acknowledged as belonging to their respective
companies.

In Easy Steps Limited supports The Forest Stewardship Council (FSC),
the leading international forest certification organisation. All our titles
that are printed on Greenpeace approved FSC certified paper carry the
FSC logo.

MIX
Paper from
responsible sources
FSC® C020837

Printed and bound in the United Kingdom

ISBN 978-1-84078-602-6

Contents

1 Introducing OS X Mavericks   7

About OS X Mavericks	8
Installing OS X Mavericks	9
The OS X Environment	10
Aqua Interface	11
About Your Mac	12
About System Preferences	17
Changing the Background	18
Changing the Screen Saver	19
Changing the Resolution	20
Accessibility	21
The Spoken Word	23
Shutting Down	24

2 Getting Up and Running   25

Introducing the Dock	26
Apps on the Dock	27
Setting Dock Preferences	28
Stacks on the Dock	30
Dock Menus	32
Working with Dock Items	33
Trash	35
System Preferences	36
About iCloud	38
Setting up iCloud	39
Using iCloud	40
Desktop Items	42
Ejecting Items	43
Resuming	44

3 Finder   45

Working with the Finder	46
Finder Folders	47
Finder Views	49
Covers	52
Quick Look	53
Finder Toolbar	54
Finder Sidebar	55

Finder Search   56
Copying and Moving Items   57
Working with Folders   58
Finder Tabs   60
Tagging in the Finder   62
Spring-loaded Folders   64
Burnable Folders   65
Selecting Items   66
Actions Button   68
Sharing from the Finder   69
Menus   70

4   Navigating in OS X Mavericks   71

A New Way of Navigating   72
No More Scroll Bars   73
Trackpad Gestures   74
Magic Mouse Gestures   82
Multi-Touch Preferences   85
Mission Control   87
Spaces and Exposé   89

5   OS X Mavericks Apps   91

Launchpad   92
Full-Screen Apps   94
OS X Apps   96
Accessing the App Store   97
Downloading Apps   98
Finding Apps   100
Managing Your Apps   102
Sharing Apps   104

6   Getting Productive   105

Dashboard   106
Spotlight Search   107
Contacts (Address Book)   108
Calendar   110
Taking Notes   112
Setting Reminders   114
Notifications   116
Getting Around with Maps   118

Preview	122
Printing	123
OS X Utilities	124
Creating PDF Documents	126

7 Internet and Email 127

Getting Connected	128
Safari	132
Safari Sidebar	133
Safari Tabbed Browsing	134
Safari Top Sites	135
Safari Reader	136
Adding Bookmarks	137
Mail	138
Using Email	139
Adding Mailboxes	140
Messaging	141
FaceTime	142

8 Digital Lifestyle 143

iPhoto	144
Viewing Photos	145
Organizing Photos	146
Editing and Sharing Photos	147
iTunes	148
Managing Your Music	149
Purchasing Music	150
Adding an iPod	151
Reading with iBooks	152
Movies, Music and Games	154

9 Sharing OS X 155

Adding Users	156
Deleting Users	158
Fast User Switching	159
OS X for the Family	160
Parental Controls	161
OS X for Windows Users	164

10 Networking 165

Networking Overview 166
Network Settings 168
File Sharing 169
Connecting to a Network 170

11 Maintaining OS X 173

Time Machine 174
Disk Utility 178
System Information 179
Activity Monitor 180
Updating Software 181
Gatekeeper 182
Privacy 183
Problems with Apps 184
General Troubleshooting 185

Index 187

Introducing OS X Mavericks

1

Mavericks is the latest operating system from Apple. It is not only enjoyable and secure to use, it also has a raft of features that transform a number of traditional ways for using computers. This chapter introduces Mavericks and shows how to get started with it.

8   About OS X Mavericks

9   Installing OS X Mavericks

10   The OS X Environment

11   Aqua Interface

12   About Your Mac

17   About System Preferences

18   Changing the Background

19   Changing the Screen Saver

20   Changing the Resolution

21   Accessibility

23   The Spoken Word

24   Shutting Down

About OS X Mavericks

OS X Mavericks is the ninth version (10.9) of the operating system for Apple computers; the iMac, MacBook, Mac Mini and Mac Pro. When OS X (pronounced 'ten') was first introduced it was a major breakthrough in terms of ease of use and stability. It is based on the UNIX programming language, which is a very stable and secure operating environment and ensures that OS X is one of the most stable consumer operating systems that has ever been designed. More importantly for the user, it is also one of the most stylish and user-friendly operating systems available.

Through the previous eight versions of OS X, it has been refined and improved in terms of both performance and functionality. This process continues with OS X Mavericks, which further develops the innovations introduced by its predecessor, OS X Mountain Lion.

When OS X Mountain Lion was introduced, in 2012, it contained a range of innovative functions that were inspired by Apple's mobile devices: iPhone, iPad and iPod touch. The two main areas where the functionality of the mobile devices has been transferred to the desktop and laptop operating system are:

- The way apps can be downloaded and installed. Instead of using a disc, OS X Mavericks utilizes the Mac App Store to provide apps, which can be installed in a couple of steps.

- Options for navigating around pages and applications on a trackpad or a Magic Mouse. Instead of having to use a mouse or a traditional laptop trackpad, OS X Mavericks allows Multi-Touch Gestures that provide a range of ways for accessing apps and web pages and navigating around them.

OS X Mavericks takes the work of OS X Mountain Lion even further, by adding more features and enhancing the ones that were already there. These include versions of Maps and iBooks for OS X so that you can look up locations and find directions, and read books that you have downloaded with OS X or any other compatible devices using iBooks.

OS X Mavericks also has a raft of behind-the-scenes features to improve the areas of performance and energy-saving for Macs using this operating system. Mavericks continues the evolution of OS X so it can now embrace both the desktop and the mobile computing world.

UNIX is an operating system that has traditionally been used for large commercial mainframe computers. It is renowned for its stability and ability to be used within different computing environments.

The New icon pictured above indicates a new or enhanced feature introduced with the latest version of OS X Mavericks.

Installing OS X Mavericks

When it comes to installing OS X Mavericks you do not need to worry about an installation CD or DVD: it can be downloaded and installed directly from the online Mac App Store. New Macs will have Mavericks installed and the following range of Macs are compatible with Mavericks and can be upgraded with it.

- iMac (Mid 2007 or newer)

- MacBook (Late 2008 Aluminum, or Early 2009 or newer)

- MacBook Pro (Mid/Late 2007 or newer)

- MacBook Air (Late 2008 or newer)

- Mac Mini (Early 2009 or newer)

- Mac Pro (Early 2008 or newer)

If you want to install OS X Mavericks on an existing Mac you will need to have minimum requirements of:

- OS X Snow Leopard (version 10.6.8), OS X Lion or OS X Mountain Lion

- Intel Core 2 Duo, Core i3, Core i5, Core i7, or Xeon processor, or above

- 2GB of memory and 8GB of available storage for installation

If your Mac meets these requirements, you can download and install OS X Mavericks, for free, as follows:

OS X Mavericks is a free upgrade if you already have the Snow Leopard, Lion or Mountain Lion versions of OS X.

1 Click on this icon on the Dock to access the App Store (or select **Software Update**, see tip)

2 Locate the **OS X Mavericks** icon (this will be on the **Featured** page or within the **Productivity** category)

3 Click on the **Download** button and follow the installation instructions

To check your computer's software version and upgrade options, click on **Apple menu > Software Update** from the main Menu bar. See page 12 for details.

The OS X Environment

The first most noticeable element about OS X is its elegant user interface. This has been designed to create a user friendly graphic overlay to the UNIX operating system at the heart of OS X and it is a combination of rich colors and sharp, original graphics. The main elements that make up the initial OS X environment are:

Hot tip

The Dock is designed to help make organizing and opening items as quick and easy as possible. For a detailed look at the Dock, see Chapter Two.

NEW

Don't forget

Many of the behind-the-scenes features of OS X Mavericks are aimed at saving power on your Mac. These include time coalescing technologies for saving processing and battery power, features for saving energy when apps are not being used; power saving features in Safari for ignoring additional content provided by web page plug-ins and memory compression to make your Mac quicker and more responsive.

Apple menu   Menu bar   Windows

The Dock   Desktop

The **Apple menu** is standardized throughout OS X, regardless of the app in use

Finder	File	Edit	View	Go
About This Mac				
Software Update...				
App Store...				
System Preferences...				
Dock				▶
Location				▶
Recent Items				▶
Force Quit Finder				⌥⇧⌘⌫
Sleep				
Restart...				
Shut Down...				
Log Out Nick Vandome...				⇧⌘Q

Aqua Interface

The name given by Apple to its OS X interface is Aqua. This describes the graphical appearance of the operating system. Essentially, it is just the cosmetic appearance of the elements within the operating system, but they combine to give OS X a rich visual look and feel. Some of the main elements of the Aqua interface are:

Menus

Menus in OS X contain commands for the operating system and any relevant apps. If there is an arrow next to a command it means there are subsequent options for the item.

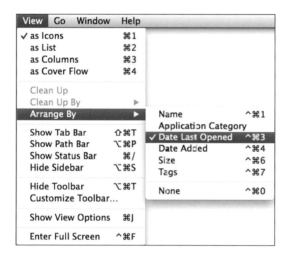

Window buttons

These appear in any open OS X window and can be used to manipulate the window.

Option buttons

Whenever a dialog box with separate options is accessed, OS X highlights the suggested option with a pulsing blue button. This can be accepted by clicking on it or by pressing Enter. If you do not want to accept this option, click on another button in the dialog box.

The graphics used in OS X are designed in a style known as Quartz. The design of this means that some elements, such as menus, allow the background behind them to show through.

The red window button is used to close a window. However, this does not quit the app. The amber button is used to minimize a window and the green one is used to expand a window.

About Your Mac

When you buy a new Mac you will almost certainly check the technical specifications before you make a purchase. Once you have your Mac, there will be times when you will want to view these specifications again, such as the version of OS X in use, the amount of memory and the amount of storage. This can be done through the About This Mac option that can be accessed from the Apple Menu. To do this:

1 Click on the **Apple Menu** and click on the **About This Mac** link

2 The **About This Mac** window has information about the version of OS X, the processor, the memory and the Startup Disk being used

3 Click on the **Software Update...** button to see available software updates for your Mac

4 Click on the **More Info...** button to view more About This Mac options

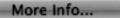

For more information about Software Updates, see page 181.

12

...cont'd

Overview
This gives additional general information about your Mac:

1 Click on the **Overview** tab

2 This window contains additional information such as the type of graphics card and the Serial Number

3 Click on the **System Report...** button to view full details about the hardware and software on your Mac

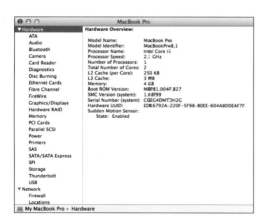

4 Click on the **Check for Updates...** button to view available software updates for your Mac

...cont'd

Display information

This gives information about your Mac's display:

1 Click on the **Displays** tab

2 This window contains information about your display including the type, size, resolution and graphics card

For more information about changing the resolution, see page 20.

3 Click on the **Displays Preferences...** button to view options for changing the display's resolution, brightness and color

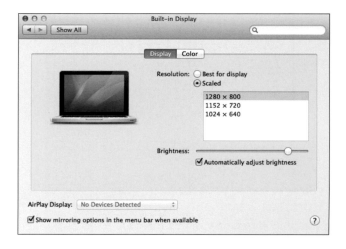

Storage information

This contains information about your Mac's physical and removable storage:

1 Click on the **Storage** tab

2 This window contains information about the used and available storage on your hard disk and also options for writing various types of CDs and DVDs

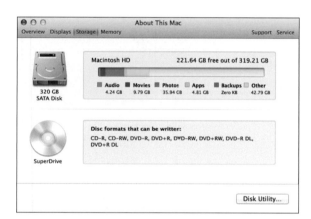

The disk usage is shown for different content types on your Mac, e.g. videos, music, photos and applications.

15

3 Click on the **Disk Utility...** button to view options for repairing problems on your Mac

...cont'd

Memory information

This contains information about your Mac's memory, which is used to run OS X and also the applications on your computer:

1 Click on the **Memory** tab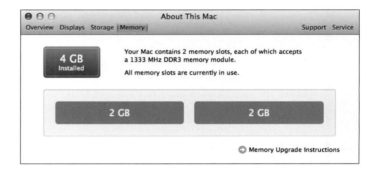

2 This window contains information about the memory chips that are in your Mac

3 Click on the **Memory Upgrade Instructions** if you want to upgrade your memory

Beware

Always wear an anti-static wristband if you are opening your Mac to insert new memory chips, or any other time when you are working on the components of your Mac.

4 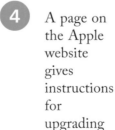 A page on the Apple website gives instructions for upgrading memory chips for different makes and models of Macs

About System Preferences

OS X Mavericks has a wide range of options for customizing and configuring the way that your Mac operates. These are located within the Systems Preferences section. To access this:

1 Click on this button on the Dock (the bar of icons that appears along the bottom of the screen), or from the Applications folder

For more detailed information about the Dock, see Chapter Two.

2 All of the options are shown in the **System Preferences** window

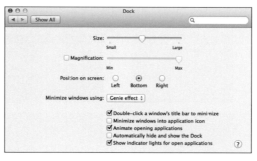

For a detailed look at the System Preferences, see pages 36-37.

3 Click once on an item to open it in the main System Preferences window. Each item will have a number of options for customization

4 Click on the **Show All** button to return to the main System Preferences window

Changing the Background

Background imagery is an important way to add your own personal touch to your Mac. (This is the graphical element upon which all other items on your computer sit.) There is a range of background options that can be used. To select your own background:

You can select your own photographs as your desktop background, once you have loaded them onto your Mac. To do this, select the iPhoto folder and browse to the photograph you want.

1 Click on this button in the **System Preferences** folder

Desktop & Screen Saver

2 Click on the **Desktop** tab

Desktop

3 Select a location from where you want to select a background

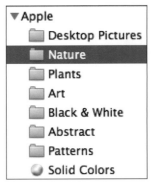

▼ Apple
📁 Desktop Pictures
📁 Nature
📁 Plants
📁 Art
📁 Black & White
📁 Abstract
📁 Patterns
⚪ Solid Colors

4 Click on one of the available backgrounds

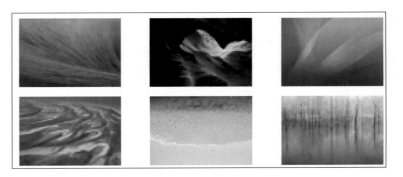

5 The background is applied as the desktop background imagery

Changing the Screen Saver

A screen saver is the element that appears when the Mac has not been used for a specified period of time. Originally this was designed to avoid screen burn (caused by items being at the same position on the screen for an extended period of time) but now they largely consist of a graphical element. To select your own screen saver:

1 Click on this button in the **System Preferences** folder

2 Click on the **Screen Saver** tab

3 Select an option here for a slideshow screen saver, or

The slideshow screen saver consists of different images that appear as tiles on the screen.

4 Scroll down to access other screen saver options

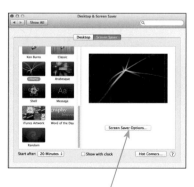

5 Click the **Screen Saver Options...** button to select options for the way the screen saver operates

Changing the Resolution

For most computer users the size at which items are displayed on the screen is a crucial issue: if items are too small this can make them hard to read and lead to eye strain; too large and you have to spend a lot of time scrolling around to see everything.

The size of items on the screen is controlled by the screen's resolution, i.e. the number of colored dots displayed in an area of the screen. The higher the resolution the smaller the items on the screen, the lower the resolution the larger the items. To change the screen resolution:

1 Click on this button in the **System Preferences** folder

2 Click on the **Display** tab

3 Click on the **Best for display** button to let your Mac select the most appropriate resolution

4 Drag this slider to change the screen brightness. Check on the box underneath it to have this done automatically

5 Click on the **Scaled** button and select a resolution setting to change the overall screen resolution

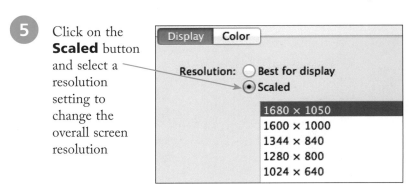

6 Click on the **Color** tab to select options for using different color profiles and also calibrating your monitor

Don't forget

A higher resolution makes items appear sharper on the screen, even though they appear physically smaller.

Accessibility

In all areas of computing it is important to give as many people access to the system as possible. This includes users with visual impairments and also people who have problems using the mouse and keyboard. In OS X this is achieved through the functions of the Accessibility System Preferences. To use these:

1 Click on this button in the **System Preferences** folder

2 Click on the **Display** button for options for changing the display colors, contrast and increasing the cursor size

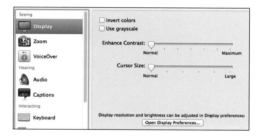

3 Click on the **Zoom** button for options to zoom in on the screen

4 Click on the **VoiceOver** button to enable VoiceOver which provides a spoken description of what is on the screen

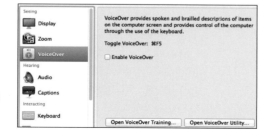

Experiment with the VoiceOver function if only to see how it operates. This will give you a better idea of how visually impaired users access information on a computer.

...cont'd

5 Click on the **Audio** button to select an on-screen flash for alerts and how sound is played

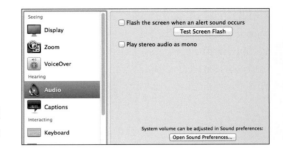

6 Click on the **Keyboard** button to access options for customizing the keyboard

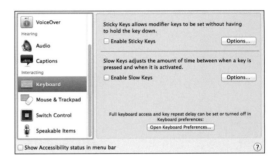

The Audio, Keyboard and Mouse & Trackpad accessibility options have links to additional options within their own System Preferences.

7 Click on the **Mouse & Trackpad** button to access options for customizing these devices

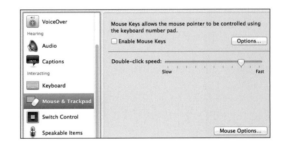

Another option in the Accessibility window is for **Switch Control**, which enables a Mac to be controlled by a variety of devices, including the mouse, keypad and gamepad devices.

8 Click on the **Speakable Items** button to select options for using spoken commands

9 Click on this button to enable assistive technology such as screen readers

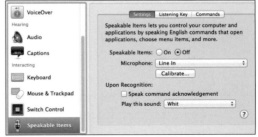

The Spoken Word

Mavericks not only has numerous options for adding text to documents, emails and messages; it also has a dictation function so that you can speak what you want to appear on screen. To set up and use the dictation feature:

1 Click on this button in the **System Preferences** folder

2 By default, Dictation is Off

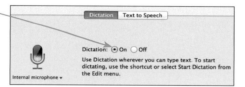

3 Click on the **On** button to enable dictation

4 Click on the **Enable Dictation** button

5 Once Dictation has been turned On, it can be accessed in relevant apps by selecting **Edit > Start Dictation** from the menu bar

6 Start talking when the microphone icon appears. Click **Done** when you have finished recording your text

7 Click on the **Text to Speech** tab to make selections for dictation

Hot tip

Punctuation can be added with the dictation function, by speaking commands such as 'comma' or 'question mark'. These will then be converted into the appropriate symbols.

Shutting Down

The Apple menu (which can be accessed by clicking on the Apple icon at the top left corner of the desktop or any subsequent OS X window) has been standardized in OS X. This means that it has the same options regardless of the app in which you are working. This has a number of advantages, not least is the fact that it makes it easier to shut down your Mac. When shutting down, there are three options that can be selected:

When shutting down, make sure you have saved all of your open documents, although OS X will prompt you to do this if you have forgotten.

24

OS X Mavericks has a **Resume** function where your Mac opens up in the same state as when you shut it down. See page 44 for details.

- **Sleep**. This puts the Mac into hibernation mode, i.e. the screen goes blank and the hard drive becomes inactive. This state is maintained until the mouse is moved or a key is pressed on the keyboard. This then wakes up the Mac and it is ready to continue work.

- **Restart**. This closes down the Mac and then restarts it again. This can be useful if you have added new software and your computer requires a restart to make it active.

- **Shut Down**. This closes down the Mac completely once you have finished working.

Click here to access the **Apple menu**

Click here to access one of the shut down options

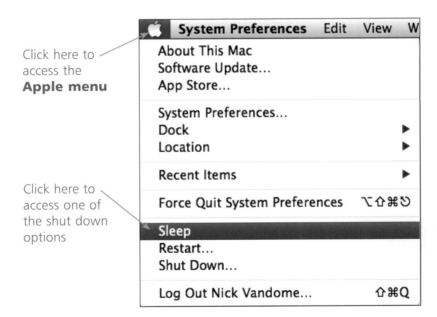

2 Getting Up and Running

This chapter looks at some of the essential features of Mavericks. These include the Dock for organizing and accessing all of the elements of your Mac computer, the system preferences for the way your Mac looks and operates and items for arranging folders and files. It also introduces the online sharing service, iCloud, for sharing your digital content.

26 Introducing the Dock

27 Apps on the Dock

28 Setting Dock Preferences

30 Stacks on the Dock

32 Dock Menus

33 Working with Dock Items

35 Trash

36 System Preferences

38 About iCloud

39 Setting up iCloud

40 Using iCloud

42 Desktop Items

43 Ejecting Items

44 Resuming

The Dock is always displayed as a line of icons, but this can be orientated either vertically or horizontally.

Items on the Dock can be opened by clicking on them once, rather than having to double-click on them. Once they have been accessed the icon bobs up and down until the item is available.

The Downloads icon can be displayed as a Folder or a Stack (see page 30). To set this, Ctrl+click on the Download icon and select either **Folder** or **Stack** under the **Display as** option.

Introducing the Dock

The Dock is one of the main organizational elements of OS X. Its main function is to help organize and access apps, folders and files. In addition, with its rich, translucent colors and elegant graphical icons, it also makes an aesthetically pleasing addition to the desktop. The main things to remember about the Dock are:

● It is divided into two: apps go on the left of the dividing line; all other items go on the right

● It can be customized in several different ways

By default, the Dock appears at the bottom of the screen

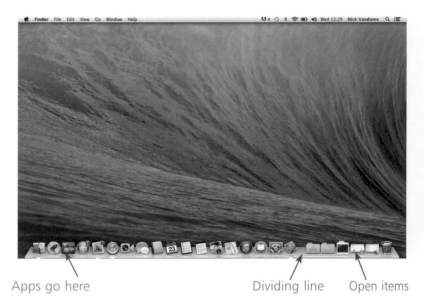

Apps go here   Dividing line   Open items

By default, the two icons to the right of the dividing line are:

Downloads. This is for items that you have downloaded from the Web. The items can be accessed from here and opened or run.

Trash. This is where items can be dragged to if you want to remove them. It can also be used to eject removable discs, such as pen drives, by dragging the device's icon over the Trash. It cannot be removed from the Dock.

Apps on the Dock

Opening apps

When you open apps they appear on the Dock and can be worked with in the Dock environment.

1 Click once on an app to open it (either on the Dock, the Finder Applications folder or the Launcher). Once an app has been opened it is displayed on the Dock, with a white mark underneath it

2 When windows are opened within the app these are displayed to the right of the dividing line

3 Click on a icon to the right of the dividing line to maximize it: it disappears from the Dock and displays at full size

4 If a window is minimized by clicking on this button, it goes back to the right-hand side of the dividing line on the Dock

5 Press and hold underneath an open app to view the available windows for the app (this will differ for different apps as some operate by using a single window)

6 To close an open app, press and hold underneath its icon on the Dock and click on the **Quit** button (or select its name on the Menu bar and select **Quit**)

Don't forget

Some apps, such as Notes, Reminders and Calendars, will close when the active window is closed. Others, such as Pages, Keynote and Numbers, will remain open even if all of the windows are closed: the recently-accessed documents will be displayed as in Step 5.

Setting Dock Preferences

As with most elements of OS X, the Dock can be modified in numerous ways. This can affect both the appearance of the Dock and the way it operates. To set Dock preferences:

Hot tip

The Apple menu is constantly available in OS X, regardless of the app in which you are working. The menu options are also constant in all apps.

1 Select **Apple menu > Dock** from the Menu bar

2 Select the general preferences here

Turn Hiding On   ⌥⌘D
Turn Magnification On

✓ Position on Left
✓ Position on Bottom
   Position on Right

Dock Preferences...

3 Click here to access more **Dock Preferences** (below)

Dock Preferences...

Beware

The Dock cannot be moved by dragging it physically; this can only be done in the Dock Preferences window.

The Dock Preferences allow you to change its size, orientation, the way icons appear and effects for when items are minimized:

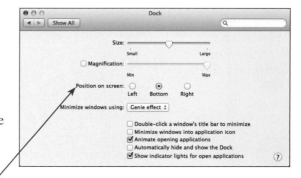

Beware

You will not be able to make the Dock size too large so that some of the icons would not be visible on the desktop. By default, the Dock is resized so that everything is always visible.

The **Position on screen** options enable you to place the Dock on the left, right or bottom of the screen

Drag the Dock **Size** slider to increase or decrease the size of the Dock

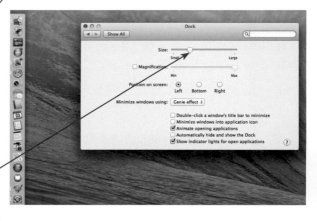

Check on the **Magnification** box and drag the slider to determine the size to which icons are enlarged when the cursor is moved over them

Move the cursor over an icon on the Dock to see the magnification effect.

The **Genie effect** under the **Minimize windows using** option shrinks the item to be minimized like a genie going back into its lamp

Hot tip

Open windows can also be minimized by double-clicking on their title bar (the thinly lined bar at the top of the window, next to the three window buttons.)

29

Manual resizing

In addition to changing the size of the Dock by using the Dock Preference dialog box, it can also be resized manually:

Drag vertically on the Dock dividing line to increase or decrease its size

Stacks on the Dock

Stacking items

To save space on the Dock it is possible to add folders to the Dock, from where their contents can be accessed. This is known as Stacks. By default, Stacks for documents and downloaded files are created on the Dock. To use Stacks:

1 Stacked items are placed on the right of the Dock dividing line

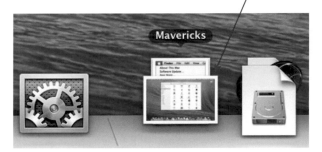

2 Click on a Stack to view its contents

3 Stacks can be viewed as a grid, or

4 As a fan, depending on the number of items it contains, or

Hot tip

Move the cursor over a stack and press Ctrl (key) + click to access options for how that stack is displayed.

5 As a list. Click on a folder to view its contents within a Stack. Click on files to open them in their relevant app

6 To create a new Stack, drag a folder onto the Dock. Any new items that are added to the folder will also be visible through the Stack

Dock Menus

One of the features of the Dock is that it can display contextual menus for selected items. This means that it shows menus with options that are applicable to the item that is being accessed. This can only be done when an item has been opened:

1 Click and hold here to display an item's individual menu

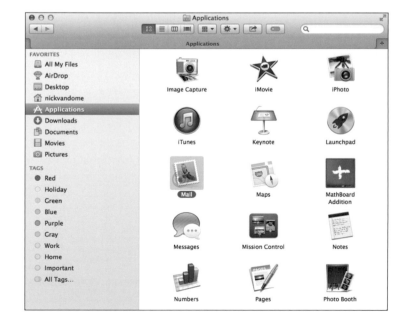

2 Click on **Show in Finder** to see where the item is located on your computer

Working with Dock Items

Adding items

As many items as you like can be added to the Dock; the only restriction is the size of monitor in which to display all of the Dock items (the size of the Dock can be reduced to accommodate more icons but you have to be careful that all of the icons are still legible). To add items to the Dock:

Locate the required item and drag it onto the Dock. All of the other icons move along to make space for the new one

Don't forget

Icons on the Dock are shortcuts to the related item, rather than the item itself, which remains in its original location.

Keep in Dock

Every time you open a new app, its icon will appear in the Dock for the duration that the program is open, even if it has not previously been put in the Dock. If you then decide that you would like to keep it in the Dock, you can do so as follows:

Beware

You can add numerous items to the Dock, but it will automatically shrink to display all of its items if it becomes too big for the available space.

1 Click and hold on the button below an open app

2 Select **Options > Keep In Dock** to ensure the app remains in the Dock when it is closed

...cont'd

Removing items

Any item, except the Finder, can be removed from the Dock. However, this does not remove it from your computer, it just removes the shortcut for accessing it. You will still be able to locate it in its folder on your hard drive and, if required, drag it back onto the Dock. To remove items from the Dock:

Drag it away from the Dock and release. The item disappears in a satisfying puff of smoke to indicate that it has been removed. All of the other icons then move up to fill in the space

Removing open apps

You can remove an app from the Dock, even if it is open and running. To do this:

1 Drag an app off the Dock while it is running. Initially the icon will remain on the Dock because the app is still open

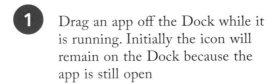

2 When the app is closed its icon will be removed from the Dock (unless Keep in Dock has been selected from the item's Dock menu)

Trash

The Trash folder is a location for placing items that you do not want to use anymore. However, when items are placed in the Trash, they are not removed from your computer. This requires another command, as the Trash is really a holding area before you decide you want to remove items permanently. The Trash can also be used for ejecting removable disks attached to your Mac.

Sending items to the Trash

Items can be sent to the Trash by dragging them from the location in which they are stored:

1 Drag an item over the **Trash** icon to place it in the Trash folder

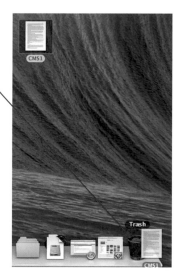

2 Click once on the **Trash** icon on the Dock to view its contents

Items can also be sent to the Trash by selecting them and then selecting **File > Move to Trash** from the Menu bar.

All of the items within the Trash can be removed in a single command: Select **Finder > Empty Trash** from the Menu bar to remove all of the items in the Trash folder.

System Preferences

In OS X there are preferences that can be set for just about every aspect of the app. This gives you great control over how the interface looks and how the operating system functions. To access System Preferences:

Click on this icon on the Dock or from the Applications folder in the Finder

Personal preferences
General. Options for the overall look of buttons, menus, windows and scroll bars.

Desktop & Screen Saver. This can be used to change the desktop background and the screen saver.

Dock. Options for the way the Dock looks and functions.

Mission Control. This gives you a variety of options for managing all of your open windows and apps.

Language & Region. Options for the language used on your Mac.

Security &Privacy. This enables you to secure your Home folder with a master password, for added security.

Spotlight. This can be used to specify settings for the OS X search facility, Spotlight.

Notifications. This can be used to set up how you are notified about items such as email, messages and software updates.

Hardware preferences
CDs & DVDs. Options for what action is taken when you insert CDs and DVDs.

Displays. Options for the screen display, such as resolution.

Energy Saver. Options for when the computer is inactive.

Keyboard. Options for how the keyboard functions and also keyboard shortcuts.

Mouse. Options for how the mouse functions.

Trackpad. Options for if you are using a trackpad.

Don't forget

OS X Mavericks supports multiple displays which means you can connect your Mac to two, or more, displays and view different content on each one. The Dock appears on the active screen and each screen also has its own menu bar. Different full screen apps can also be viewed on each screen.

Printers & Scanners. Options for selecting printers and scanners.

Sound. Options for adding sound effects and playing and recording sound.

Internet & Wireless preferences
iCloud. Options for the online iCloud service.

Internet Accounts. This can be used to set up contacts on your Mac, using a variety of online services.

Network. This can be used to specify network settings for linking two or more computers together. This is covered in more detail in Chapter 10.

Bluetooth. Options for attaching Bluetooth wireless devices.

Sharing. This can be used to specify how files are shared over a network. This is also covered in Chapter 10.

System preferences
Users & Groups. This can be used to allow different users to create their own accounts for use on the same computer.

Parental Controls. This can be used to limit access to the computer and various online functions.

App Store. This can be used to specify how software updates are handled. It connects to the App Store to access the available updates.

Dictation & Speech. Options for using speakable commands to control the computer.

Date & Time. Options for changing the computer's date and time to time zones around the world.

Startup Disk. This can be used to specify the disk from which your computer starts up. This is usually the OS X volume.

Time Machine. This can be used to configure and set up the OS X backup facility.

Accessibility. This can be used to set options for users who have difficulty with viewing text on screen, hearing commands, using the keyboard or using the mouse.

The **Internet Accounts** section can be used to set up email accounts and also link to your social networking accounts such as Facebook, Twitter and LinkedIn.

About iCloud

Cloud computing is an attractive proposition and one that has gained greatly in popularity in recent years. As a concept, it consists of storing your content on an external computer server. This not only gives you added security in terms of backing up your information, it also means that the content can then be shared over a variety of mobile devices.

iCloud is Apple's consumer cloud computing product that consists of online services such as email, a calendar, notes, contacts and saving documents. iCloud provides users with a way to save their files and content to the online service and then use them across their Apple devices such as other Mac computers, iPhones, iPads and iPod Touches.

About iCloud

iCloud can be set up from this icon within System Preferences:

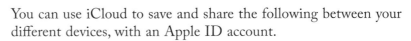

You can use iCloud to save and share the following between your different devices, with an Apple ID account.

- Music

- Photos

- Documents

- Apps

- Books

- Backups

- Contacts, calendar, notes and reminders

When you save an item to the iCloud it automatically pushes it to all of your other compatible devices; you do not have to manually sync anything, iCloud does it all for you.

The standard iCloud service is free and this includes an iCloud email address and 5GB of online storage.(*Correct at the time of printing.*)

There is also a version of iCloud for Windows.

Setting up iCloud

To use iCloud with Mavericks you need to first have an Apple ID. This is a service you can register for to be able to access a range of Apple facilities, including iCloud. You can register with an email address and a password. When you first start using iCloud you will be prompted for your Apple ID details. If you do not have an Apple ID you can apply for one at this point:

① Sign in with your Apple ID, or

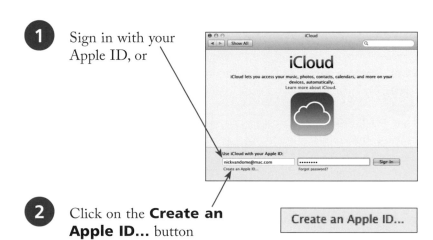

Don't forget

To use iTunes and iPhoto with iCloud, you need to have iTunes 10.5, or later, and iPhoto 9.2, or later, in order to share your music and photos.

② Click on the **Create an Apple ID...** button

Create an Apple ID...

Setting up iCloud
To use iCloud:

① Open System Preferences and click on the **iCloud** button

iCloud

② Check on the items you want included within iCloud. All of these items will be backed up and shared across all of your Apple devices

Don't forget

Music and photos are not included in your 5GB storage limit on iCloud. This only includes emails, documents, account information, Camera Roll (for saved or edited photos) and account settings. Photos in Photo Stream are stored in iCloud, but this is not part of the storage limit. Music is stored via iTunes.

Using iCloud

Once iCloud has been set up in System Preferences there is relatively little that needs to be done. iCloud will take care of things in the background and backup and share all of the items that have been specified. For instance, when you create a note or a reminder it will be saved by iCloud and made available to any other Apple devices that are iCloud-enabled. Photos and documents can also be shared via iCloud.

Sharing photos

Photos can be shared via iCloud using the iPhoto app:

Hot tip

Once you have set up iCloud, you can login to the online service at **www.icloud.com/** This includes your online email service, contacts, calendar, reminders, notes and versions of Pages, Keynote and Numbers. You can log in to your iCloud account from any Internet-enabled device.

1 When iCloud is active, a Photo Stream folder is created in iPhoto under the **Shared > iCloud** button

Hot tip

When you import new photos into iPhoto these are added to the Photo Stream (providing you have an Internet connection). To use existing photos in iPhoto, just drag them from the main window onto the Photo Stream button.

2 All of the photos in the Photo Stream will be available in other iCloud-enabled devices. Similarly, you will be able to view the Photo Streams from your other devices

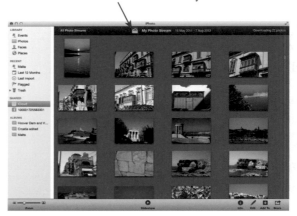

Sharing documents

The latest versions of the Apple productivity apps (Pages, Numbers and Keynote) are optimized for use with iCloud. This means that if you create a presentation or report on, for instance, an iPad, you can also open it on a Mac running Mavericks (as long as you have the same apps). To share documents:

Pages is the Apple app for word processing, Numbers for spreadsheets and Keynote for presentations. These can all be downloaded from the App Store.

1 In the iCloud System Preferences, make sure that the **Documents & Data** option is checked On

2 Open one of the Apple productivity apps, such as Pages

3 Click on the **iCloud** button to view which documents are available in the iCloud. Click on the **On My Mac** button to see which documents are just on your Mac

4 Open and edit a document from the iCloud. The edited document will then be available on other iCloud-enabled devices

Another useful iCloud function is the iCloud Keychain (**System Preferences > iCloud** and check on the **Keychain** option.) If this is enabled, it can keep all of your passwords and credit card information up-to-date across multiple devices and remember them when you use them on websites. The information is encrypted and controlled through your Apple ID.

5 Click next to the document title at the top of the window. Make sure that iCloud is selected in the **Where** box and click on **File > Save** from the menu bar

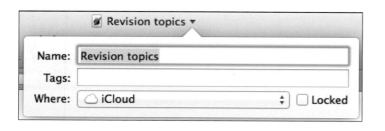

Desktop Items

If required, the Desktop can be used to store apps and files. However, the Finder (see Chapter Three) does such a good job of organizing all of the elements within your computer that the Desktop is rendered largely redundant, unless you feel happier storing items here. The Desktop also displays any removable disks that are connected to your computer:

Icons for removable disks, e.g. pen drives, CDs or DVDs, will only become visible on the Desktop once a disk has been inserted into the appropriate drive.

42

If a removable disk is connected to your computer, double-click the Desktop icon to view its contents

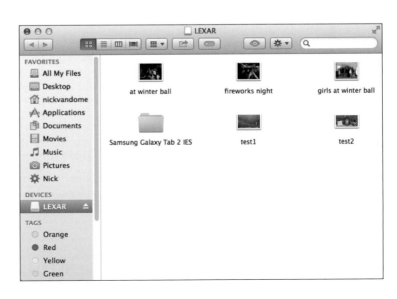

Any removable disks that are connected to your computer can also be viewed by clicking on them in the Sidebar in the Finder.

Ejecting Items

If you have removable disks attached to your Mac it is essential to be able to eject them quickly and easily. In OS X there are two ways in which this can be done:

1 In the Finder, click on the icon to the right of the name of the removable disk

2 On the Desktop, drag the disk icon over the **Trash**. This turns the Trash icon into the **Eject** icon and the disk will be ejected

3 Some discs, such as CDs and DVDs, are physically ejected when either of these two actions are performed. Other disks, such as pen drives, have to be removed manually once they have been ejected by OS X. If the disk is not ejected first the following warning message will appear:

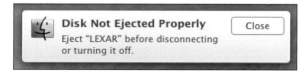

Resuming

One of the chores about computing is that when you close down your computer you have to first close down all of your open documents and apps and then open them all again when you turn your machine back on again. However, OS X Mavericks has an innovative feature that allows you to continue working exactly where you left off, even if you turn off your computer. To do this:

1 Before you close down, all of your open documents and apps are available (as shown)

2 Select the **Shut Down** or **Restart** option from the **Apple menu**

3 Make sure this box is checked on (this will ensure that all of your items will appear as before once the Mac is closed down and then opened again)

4 Confirm the **Shut Down** or **Restart** command

3 Finder

The principal method for moving around OS X Mavericks is the Finder. This enables you to access items and organize your apps, folders and files. This chapter looks at how to use the Finder and how to get the most out of this powerful tool that is at the heart of navigating around OS X. It covers accessing items through the Finder, how to customize the interface and numerous options for working with folders in OS X Mavericks.

46 Working with the Finder

47 Finder Folders

49 Finder Views

52 Covers

53 Quick Look

54 Finder Toolbar

55 Finder Sidebar

56 Finder Search

57 Copying and Moving Items

58 Working with Folders

60 Finder Tabs

62 Tagging in the Finder

64 Spring-loaded Folders

65 Burnable Folders

66 Selecting Items

68 Actions Button

69 Sharing from the Finder

70 Menus

Working with the Finder

If you were only able to use one item on the Dock it would be the Finder. This is the gateway to all of the elements of your computer. It is possible to get to selected items through other routes, but the Finder is the only location where you can gain access to everything on your system. If you ever feel that you are getting lost within OS X, click on the Finder and then you should begin to feel more at home. To access the Finder:

Click once on this icon on the Dock

Overview

The Finder has its own toolbar; a Sidebar from which items can be accessed and a main window where the contents of selected items can be viewed:

Forward and back   View options   Actions button   Search

View all files

Folders are displayed here in the Sidebar

Tags

Main windows

Finder Folders

All My Files

This contains all of the latest files on which you have been working. They are sorted into categories according to file type so that you can search through them quickly. This is an excellent way to locate items without having to look through a lot of folders. To access this:

1 Click on this link in the Finder Sidebar to access the contents of your **All My Files** folder

2 All of your files are displayed in individual categories

The Finder is always open (as denoted by the graphic underneath its icon on the Dock) and it cannot readily be closed down or removed.

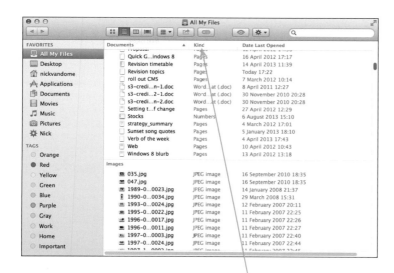

3 Click on the headings at the top of each category to sort items by that criteria

...cont'd

Home folder

This contains the contents of your own home directory, containing your personal folders and files. OS X inserts some pre-named folders which it thinks will be useful, but it is possible to rename, rearrange or delete these as you please. It is also possible to add as many more folders as you want:

1 Click on this link to access the contents of your **Home** folder

2 The Home folder contains the **Public** folder that can be used to share files with other users if the computer is part of a network

Applications

This folder contains all of the applications on your Mac. They can also be accessed from the Launchpad as shown in Chapter Five.

Documents

This is part of your home folder but is put on the Finder Sidebar for ease of access. New folders can be created for different types of documents.

48

Hot tip

When you are creating documents, OS X by default, recognizes their type and then, when you save them, suggests the most applicable folder in your Home directory in which to save them. So, if you have created a word processed document, OS X will suggest you save it in Documents, if it is a photograph it will suggest Pictures, if it is a video it will suggest Movies, and so on.

Finder Views

The way in which items are displayed within the Finder can be amended in a variety of ways, depending on how you want to view the contents of a folder. Different folders can have their own viewing options applied to them and these will stay in place until a new option is specified.

Back button

When working within the Finder each new window replaces the previous one, unless you open a new program. This prevents the screen becoming cluttered with dozens of open windows, as you look through various Finder windows for a particular item. To ensure that you never feel lost within the Finder structure, there is a Back button on the Finder toolbar that enables you to retrace the steps that you have taken:

If you have not opened any Finder windows, the Back button will not operate.

1 Navigate to a folder within the Finder (in this case the **Croatia** folder contained within **Pictures**)

Select an item within the Finder window and click on the space bar to view its details.

2 Click on the **Back** button to move back to the previously-visited window (in this case, the main **Pictures** window)

...cont'd

Icon view

One of the viewing options for displaying items within the Finder is as icons. This provides a graphical representation of the items in the Finder. It is possible to customize the way that Icon view looks and functions:

The Arrange By options can be used to arrange icons into specific groups, e.g. by name or type, or to snap them to an invisible grid so that they have an ordered appearance.

A very large icon size can be useful for people with poor eyesight, but it does take up a lot more space in a window.

1 Click here on the Finder toolbar to access **Icon** view

2 Select **View** from the Menu bar, check on **as Icons** and select **Show View Options** to access the options for customizing Icon view

Drag this slider to set the icon size

Select an option for the way icons are arranged in Finder windows

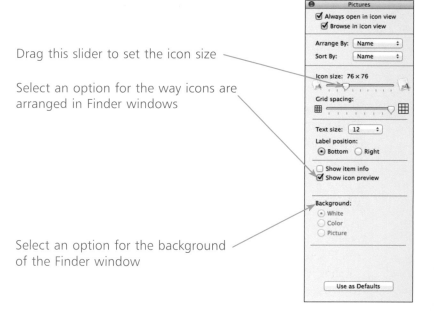

Select an option for the background of the Finder window

List view

List view can be used to show the items within a Finder window as a list, with additional information shown next to them. This can be a more efficient method than Icon view if there are a lot of items within a folder, as List view enables you to see more items at one time and also view the additional information:

1 Click here on the Finder toolbar to access **List** view

2 The name of each folder or file is displayed here. If any item has additional elements within it, this is represented by a small triangle next to it. Additional information in List view, such as file size and last modified date, is included in columns to the right

List view can be customized to include a variety of information such as file size and date last modified.

51

Column view

Column view is a useful option if you want to trace the location of a particular item, i.e. see the full path of its location, starting from the hard drive:

1 Click here on the Finder toolbar to access **Column** view

2 Click on an item to see everything within that folder. If an arrow follows an item it means that there are further items to view

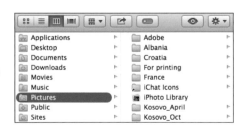

Covers

Covers is another innovative feature on the Mac, that enables you to view items as large icons. This is particularly useful for image files as it enables you to quickly see the details of the image to see if it is the one you want. To use Covers:

1   Select a folder and at the top of the Finder window click on this button

2   The items within the folder are displayed in their cover state

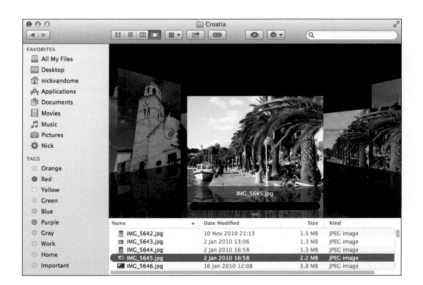

3   Drag with the mouse on each item to view the next one, or click on the slider at the bottom of the window. You can also move between items by swiping left or right on a trackpad or Magic Mouse

Quick Look

Through a Finder option called Quick Look, it is possible to view the content of a file without having to first open it. To do this:

1 Select a file within the Finder

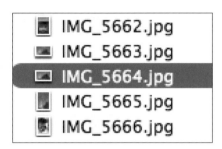

2 Press the space bar

3 The contents of the file are displayed without it opening in its default program

4 Click on the cross to close Quick Look

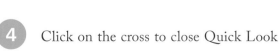

Hot tip

In Quick Look it is even possible to preview videos or presentations without having to first open them in their default program.

Finder Toolbar

Customizing the toolbar

As with most elements of OS X, it is possible to customize the Finder toolbar:

Beware

Do not put too many items on the Finder toolbar, because you may not be able to see them all in the Finder window. If there are additional toolbar items, there will be a directional arrow indicating this. Click on the arrow to view the available items.

1 Select **View > Customize Toolbar...** from the Menu bar

2 Drag items from the window into the toolbar, or

3 Drag the default set of icons into the toolbar

4 Click **Done** at the bottom of the window

54

Finder Sidebar

Using the Sidebar

The Sidebar is the left-hand panel of the Finder which can be used to access items on your Mac:

1 Click on a button on the Sidebar

2 Its contents are displayed in the main Finder window

Adding to the Sidebar

Items that you access most frequently can be added to the Sidebar. To do this:

1 Drag an item from the main Finder window onto the Sidebar

2 The item is added to the Sidebar. You can do this with apps, folders and files

Finder Search

Searching electronic data is now a massive industry, with companies such as Google leading the way with online searching. On Macs it is also possible to search your folders and files, using the built-in search facilities. This can be done either through the Finder or with the Spotlight program (see page 107).

Using Finder

To search for items within the Finder:

Don't forget

Try and make your search keywords and phrases as accurate as possible. This will create a better list of search results.

1 In the Finder window, enter the search keyword(s) in this box. Search options are listed below the keyword

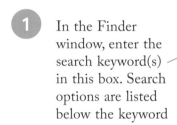

2 Select an option for what you want to search over

3 In the Search box click on the token next to the keyword. This gives you additional options for what to search over

4 The search results are shown in the Finder window

Don't forget

Both folders and files will be displayed in the Finder as part of the search results.

5 Double-click on a file to open it

Copying and Moving Items

Items can be copied and moved within OS X by using the copy and paste method or by dragging:

Copy and paste

1 Select an item and select **Edit > Copy** from the Menu bar

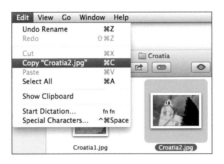

57

When an item is copied, it is placed on the Clipboard and remains there until another item is copied.

2 Move to the target location and select **Edit > Paste Item** from the Menu bar. The item is then pasted into the new location

Dragging
Drag a file from one location into another to move it to that location

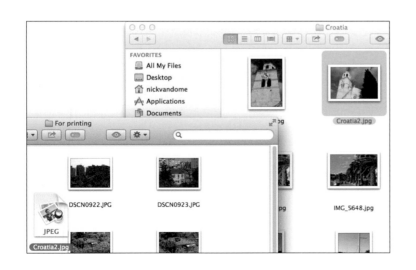

Hold down the Option key while dragging to copy an item rather than moving it.

Working with Folders

When OS X is installed, there are various folders that have already been created to hold apps and files. Some of these are essential (i.e. those containing apps) while others are created as an aid for where you might want to store the files that you create (such as the Pictures and Movies folders). Once you start working with OS X you will probably want to create your own folders, in which to store and organize your documents. This can be done on the desktop or within any level of your existing folder structure. To create a new folder:

1 Access the location in which you want to create the new folder (e.g. your Home folder) and select **File > New Folder** from the Menu bar

2 A new, empty, folder is inserted at the selected location (named "untitled folder")

Don't forget

Folders are always denoted by a folder icon. This is the same regardless of the Finder view which is selected. The only difference is that the icon is larger in Icon view than in List or Column views.

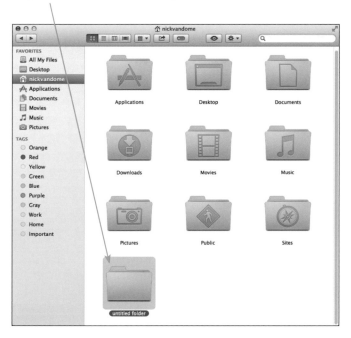

3 Overtype the file name with a new one. Press **Enter**

You can create as many "nested" folders (i.e. folders within other folders) as you want. However, this makes your folder structure more complicated and, after time, you may forget where all your folders are and what they contain.

4 Double-click on a folder to view its contents (at this point it should be empty)

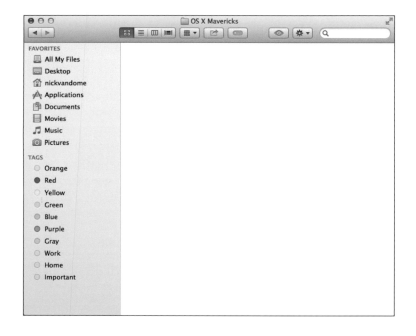

Content can be added to an empty folder by dragging it from another folder and dropping it into the new one.

Finder Tabs

Tabs in web browsers are now well established, where you can have several pages open within the same browser window. This technology now comes to the Finder in OS X Mavericks with the introduction of Finder Tabs. This enables different folders to be open in different tabs within the Finder so that you can organize your content exactly how you want. To do this:

1 Select **View > Show Tab Bar** from the Finder menu bar

2 A new tab is opened at the right-hand side of the Finder

Don't forget

Each time a new tab is opened it displays the contents of the **All My Files** window, regardless of what is displayed in the previous tab window.

3 Click on this button to view the new tab

4 At this point the content in the new tab is displayed for the **All My Files** window

5 Access a new folder to display this as the content for the tab. In this way you can use different tabs for different types of content, such as photos or music, or for different topics such as Work, Travel or Finance within Documents

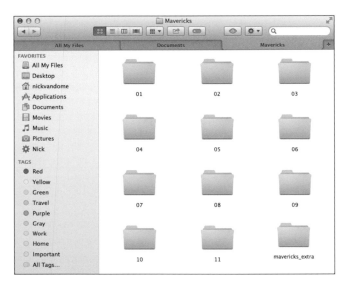

Dozens of tabs can be added in the Finder. However, when there are too many to fit along the Tab Bar they are stacked on top of each other, so it is hard to work out what you have in your tabs.

6 Each tab view can be customized and this is independent of the other tabs

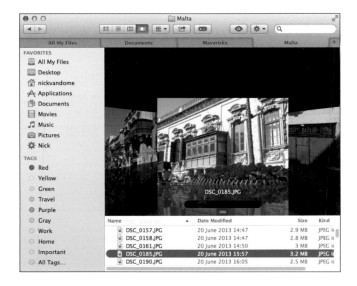

Tagging in the Finder

When creating content in OS X Mavericks you may find that you have documents of different types that cover the same topic. For instance, you may have work-related documents in Pages for reports, Keynote for presentations and Numbers for spreadsheets. With the Finder Tags function it is possible to link related content items through the use of colored tags. These can be added to items in the Finder and also in apps when content is created.

1 The tags are listed in the Finder Sidebar

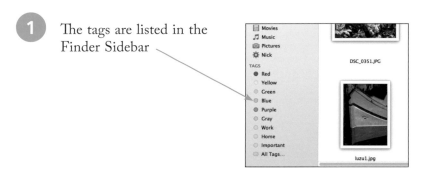

2 To give tags specific names, Ctrl + click on one and click on the **Rename** link

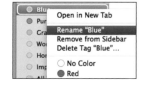

Tags can also be added to items by Ctrl + clicking on them and selecting the required tag from the menu that appears. Also, they can be added from this button on the main Finder toolbar.

3 To add tags, select the required items in the Finder window

4 Drag the selected items over the appropriate tag

5 The tags are added to the selected items

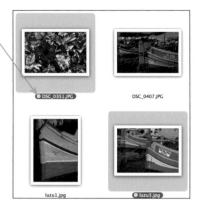

Adding tags in apps

Tags can also be added when documents are created in certain apps, such as Pages, Keynote and Numbers:

1 Select **File > Save**, click in the **Tags** box and select the required tag. Click on the **Save** button

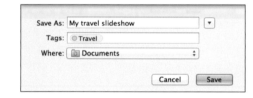

Tags can also be added to iCloud documents so that when you are viewing content in iCloud, all tagged items can be viewed together.

Viewing tags

To view all documents that have had the same tag added:

1 Click on the required tag in the Finder Sidebar. All of the tagged documents will be displayed, regardless of their content type, or where they are saved on your Mac

63

Spring-loaded Folders

Another method for moving items with the Finder is to use the spring-loaded folder option. This enables you to drag items into a folder and then view the contents of the folder before you drop the item into it. This means that you can drag items into nested folders in a single operation. To do this:

1 Select the item you want to move

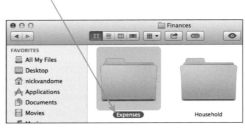

2 Drag the selected item over the folder into which you want to place it. Keep the mouse held down

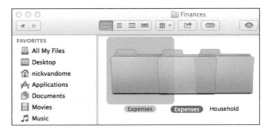

3 The folder will open, revealing its contents. The selected item can either be dropped into the folder or, if there are sub-folders, the same operation can be repeated until you find the folder into which you want to place the selected item. Release the item to complete the operation

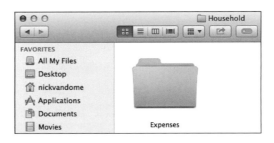

Burnable Folders

With the increasing use of images, digital video and music files, computer users are frequently copying data from their computers onto CDs. In some cases this can be a frustrating process but in OS X the use of burnable folders can make the process much quicker. These are folders that can be created specifically for the contents to be burned onto a CD or DVD. To do this:

1 In the Finder, select **File > New Burn Folder** from the Menu bar

65

Hot tip

Applications such as iTunes and iPhoto can be used to burn CDs using the content within that application, but burnable folders are the best way to combine files from a variety of different applications and then burn them onto discs.

2 The burn folder is created in the Finder window which was active when Step 1 was performed. Click on the folder name and overtype to give it a unique name

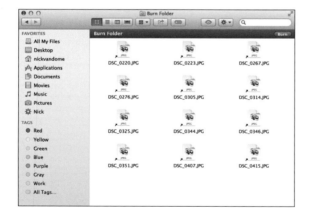

3 Select the items that you want to burn and drag and drop or copy and paste them into the burn folder

4 Click here to burn the disc

Selecting Items

Apps and files within OS X folders can be selected by a variety of different methods.

Selecting by dragging

Drag the cursor to encompass the items to be selected. The selected items will become highlighted.

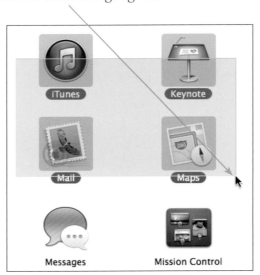

Once items have been selected, a single command can be applied to all of them. For instance, you can copy a group of items by selecting them and then applying the Copy command from the Menu bar.

Selecting by clicking

Click once on an item to select it, hold down Shift and then click on another item in a list to select a consecutive group of items.

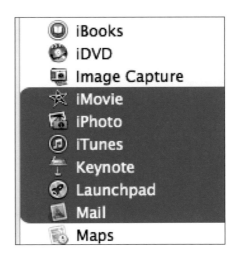

To select a non-consecutive group, select the first item by clicking on it once, then hold down the Command key (⌘) and select the other required items. The selected items will appear highlighted.

The Select All command selects all of the elements within the active item. For instance, if the active item is a word processing document, the Select All command will select all of the items within the document; if it is a folder it will select all of the items within that folder.

Select All

To select all of the items in a folder, select **Edit > Select All** from the Menu bar.

Edit	View	Go	Window	Help
Undo				⌘Z
Redo				⇧⌘Z
Cut				⌘X
Copy				⌘C
Paste				⌘V
Select All				⌘A
Show Clipboard				
Start Dictation				fn fn
Special Characters...				^⌘Space

Actions Button

The Finder Actions button provides a variety of options for any item, or items, selected in the Finder. To use this:

1 Select an item, or group of items, about which you want to find out additional information

If an image has been selected, the Actions button can be used to set it as the Desktop Picture, by selecting this option at the bottom of the Actions menu.

2 Click on the **Actions** button on the Finder toolbar

68

3 The available options for the selected item, or items, are displayed. These include **Get Summary Info** which displays additional information about an item, such as file type, file size, creation and modification dates and the default program for opening the item

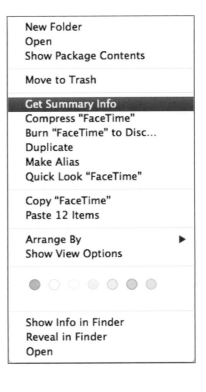

The Actions button can also be used for labeling items with Finder Tags. To do this, select the required items in the Finder and click on the colored tags at the bottom of the Actions button menu. The selected tag will be applied to the item names in the Finder.

Sharing from the Finder

Next but one to the Actions button on the Finder is the Share button. This can be used to share a selected item, or items, in a variety of ways appropriate to the type of file that has been selected. For instance, a photo will have options including the photo sharing site Flickr while a text document will have fewer options. To share items directly from the Finder:

1 Locate and select the item(s) that you want to share

brittany_church2.jpg

Don't forget

Another button on the Finder is for changing the arrangement of items within the Finder. Click on this button to access arrangement options such as Name, Date and Size.

2 Click on the **Share** button on the Finder toolbar and select one of the options

- Email
- Messages
- Twitter
- Facebook
- Flickr

3 For some of the options, such as Twitter and Flickr, you will be asked to add an account. If you already have an account with these services you can enter the details or, if not, you can create a new account

Hot tip

You can also add your social networking accounts from **System Preferences > Internet Accounts**. Select the required account and enter your login details.

Twitter

No account is configured

Cancel   Add Account...

Menus

The main Apple menu bar in OS X Mavericks contains a variety of menus, which are accessed when the Finder is the active window. When individual apps are open they have their own menu bars, although in a lot of cases these are similar to the standard menu bar, particularly for the built-in OS X Mavericks apps such as the Calendar, Contacts and Notes.

- **Apple menu.** This is denoted by a translucent blue apple and contains general information about the computer, a preferences option for changing the functionality and appearance of the Dock and options for closing down the computer.

- **Finder menu.** This contains preferences options for amending the functionality and appearance of the Finder and also options for emptying the Trash and accessing other apps (under the Services option).

- **File menu.** This contains common commands for working with open documents, such as opening and closing files, creating aliases, moving to the Trash, ejecting external devices and burning discs.

- **Edit menu.** This contains common commands that apply to the majority of apps used on the Mac. These include undo, cut, copy, paste, select all and show the contents of the clipboard, i.e. items that have been cut or copied.

- **View.** This contains options for how windows and folders are displayed within the Finder and for customizing the Finder toolbar. This includes showing or hiding the Finder Sidebar and selecting view options for the size at which icons are displayed within Finder windows.

- **Go.** This can be used to navigate around your computer. This includes moving to your All My Files folder, your Home folder, your Applications folder and recently accessed folders.

- **Window.** This contains commands to organize the currently open apps and files on your desktop.

- **Help.** This contains the Mac Help files which contain information about all aspects of OS X Mavericks.

4 Navigating in OS X Mavericks

OS X Mavericks has multi-touch gestures for navigating around your apps and documents. This chapter looks at how to use this to best get around your Mac.

72 A New Way of Navigating

73 No More Scroll Bars

74 Trackpad Gestures

82 Magic Mouse Gestures

85 Multi-Touch Preferences

87 Mission Control

89 Spaces and Exposé

Don't forget

If you do not have a trackpad, a Magic Trackpad or a Magic Mouse you can still navigate in Mavericks with a traditional mouse and the use of scroll bars in windows.

A New Way of Navigating

One of the most revolutionary features of OS X Lion, which is continued with Mavericks, is the way in which you can navigate around your applications, web pages and documents. This involves a much greater reliance on swiping on a trackpad or adapted mouse; techniques that have been imported from the iPhone and the iPad. These are known as Multi-Touch Gestures and to take full advantage of these you will need to have one of the following devices:

- **A trackpad.** This will be found on new MacBooks.

- **A Magic Trackpad.** This can be used with an iMac, a Mac Mini or a Mac Pro. It works wirelessly via Bluetooth.

- **A Magic Mouse.** This can be used with an iMac, a Mac Mini or a Mac Pro. It works wirelessly via Bluetooth.

All of these devices work using a swiping technique with fingers moving over their surface. This should be done with a light touch; it is a gentle swipe, rather than any pressure being applied to the device.

The trackpads and Magic Mouse do not have any buttons in the same way as traditional devices. Instead, specific areas are clickable so that you can still perform left- and right-click operations.

On a Magic Mouse the center and right side can be used for clicking operations and on a Magic Trackpad the left and right corners can perform the same tasks.

No More Scroll Bars

Another feature in Mavericks is the removal of scroll bars that are constantly visible on a web page or document. Instead, there are scroll bars that only appear when you are moving around a page or document. When you stop, the scroll bars melt away. Scrolling is done by Multi-Touch Gestures on a Magic Trackpad, a trackpad or a Magic Mouse and these gestures are looked at on the following pages. To perform scrolling with Mavericks:

1 Scroll around a web page or document by swiping up or down on a Magic Mouse, a Magic Trackpad, or a trackpad. As you move up or down the scroll bar appears

Web pages and document windows can also be navigated around by dragging on the scroll bars using a mouse or a trackpad.

2 When you stop scrolling the bar disappears, to allow optimum viewing area for your web page or document

Trackpad Gestures

Pointing and clicking

A Magic Trackpad, or trackpad, can be used to perform a variety of pointing and clicking tasks:

1 Tap with one finger in the middle of the Magic Trackpad, or trackpad, to perform a single click operation, e.g. to click on a button or click on an open window

2 Tap once with two fingers in the middle of the Magic Trackpad, or trackpad, to access any contextual menus associated with an item (this is the equivalent of the traditional right-click with a mouse)

3 Highlight a word or phrase and double-tap with three fingers to see look-up information for the selected item. This is frequently a dictionary definition but it can also be a Wikipedia entry

If you have too many functions set using the same number of fingers, some of them may not work. See pages 85-86 for details about setting preferences for Multi-Touch Gestures.

4 Move over an item and drag with three fingers to move the item around the screen

...cont'd

Scrolling and zooming

One of the most common operations on a computer is scrolling on a page, whether it is a web page or a document. Traditionally, this has been done with a mouse and a cursor. However, using a Magic Trackpad you can now do all of your scrolling with your fingers. There are a number of options for doing this.

Scrolling up and down

To move up and down web pages or documents, use two fingers on the Magic Trackpad, or trackpad, and swipe up or down. The page moves in the opposite direction to the one in which you are swiping, i.e. if you swipe up, the page moves down and vice versa:

Don't worry if you cannot immediately get the hang of Multi-Touch Gestures. It takes a bit of practice to get the correct touch and pressure on the Magic Trackpad, a trackpad or the Magic Mouse.

1 Open a web page

2 Position two fingers in the middle of the Magic Trackpad, or trackpad

3 Swipe them up to move down the page

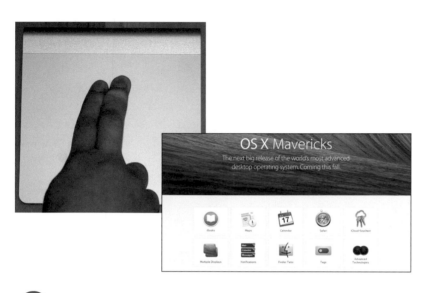

When scrolling up and down pages, the gesture moves the page the opposite way, i.e. swipe down to move up the page and vice versa.

4 Swipe them down to move up a page

...cont'd

Zooming in and out

To zoom in or out on web pages or documents:

1 To zoom in, position your thumb and forefinger in the middle of the Magic Trackpad, or trackpad

Pages can also be zoomed in on by double-tapping with two fingers.

2 Spread them outwards to zoom in on a web page or document

...cont'd

3 To zoom out, position your thumb and forefinger at opposite corners of the Magic Trackpad, or trackpad

There is a limit on how far you can zoom in or out on a web page or document, to ensure that it does not distort the content too much.

4 Swipe them into the center of the Magic Trackpad, or trackpad, to zoom out

...cont'd

Moving between pages

With Multi-Touch Gestures it is possible to swipe between pages within a document. To do this:

1 Position two fingers to the left or right of the Magic Trackpad, or trackpad

2 Swipe to the opposite side of the Magic Trackpad, or trackpad, to move through the document

Don't forget

See pages 94-95 for details about using full-screen apps.

Moving between full-screen apps

In addition to moving between pages by swiping, it is also possible to move between different apps when they are in full-screen mode. To do this:

1 Position three fingers to the left or right of the Magic Trackpad, or trackpad

2 Swipe to the opposite side of the Magic Trackpad, or trackpad, to move through the available full-screen apps

Showing the Desktop

To show the whole Desktop, regardless of how many files or apps are open:

1 Position your thumb and three fingers in the middle of the Magic Trackpad, or trackpad

2 Swipe to the opposite corners cf the Magic Trackpad, or trackpad, to display the Desktop

3 The Desktop is displayed, with all items minimized around the side of the screen

Magic Mouse Gestures

Pointing and clicking

A Magic Mouse can be used to perform a variety of pointing and clicking tasks:

1 Click with one finger on the Magic Mouse to perform a single-click operation, e.g. to select a button or command

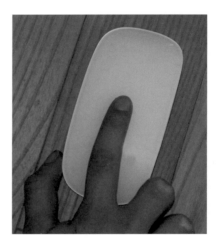

2 Tap with one finger on the right side of the Magic Mouse to access any contextual menus associated with an item (this is the equivalent of the traditional right-click with a mouse)

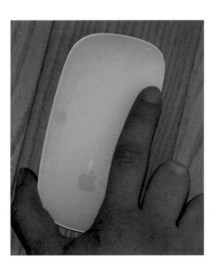

Don't forget

The right-click operation can be set within the Mouse System Preferences.

...cont'd

Scrolling and zooming
The Magic Mouse can also be used to perform scrolling and zooming functions within a web page or document:

1 Swipe up or down with one finger to move up and down a web page or document

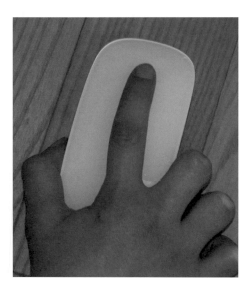

When scrolling on a web page or document, it moves in the opposite direction to the movement of your finger, i.e. if you swipe up, the page moves down and vice versa.

Don't forget

2 Double-tap with one finger to zoom in on a web page

...cont'd

3 Swipe left or right with one finger to move between pages

4 Swipe left or right with two fingers to move between full-screen apps

Multi-Touch Preferences

Some Multi-Touch Gestures only have a single action, which cannot be changed. However, others have options for changing the action for a specific gesture. This is done within the respective preferences for the Magic Mouse, the Magic Trackpad or the trackpad, where a full list of Multi-Touch Gestures is shown. To use these:

1 Access the System Preferences and click on the **Mouse** or **Trackpad** button

Mouse

2 Click on one of the tabs at the top

More Gestures

3 The actions are described on the left, with a graphic explanation on the right

Don't forget

The Magic Trackpad, or trackpad, has three tabbed options within the System Preferences: Point & Click, Scroll & Zoom and More Gestures. The Magic Mouse has preferences for Point & Click and More Gestures.

85

4 If there is a down arrow next to an option, click on it to change the way an action is activated

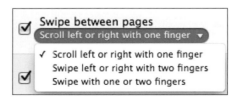

...cont'd

Trackpad Gestures

The full list of Trackpad Multi-Touch Gestures, with their default action are (relevant ones for Magic Mouse are in brackets):

Point & Click

- Tap to click – tap once with one finger (same for the Magic Mouse)

- Secondary click – click or tap with two fingers (single-click on the right of the Magic Mouse)

- Look up – double-tap with three fingers

- Three finger drag – move with three fingers

Scroll & Zoom

- Scroll direction: natural – content tracks finger movement, with two fingers (one finger with the Magic Mouse)

- Zoom in or out – pinch or spread with two fingers

- Smart zoom – double-tap with two fingers (double-tap with one finger with the Magic Mouse)

- Rotate – rotate with two fingers

More Gestures

- Swipe between pages – scroll left or right with two fingers (scroll left or right with one finger with the Magic Mouse)

- Swipe between full-screen apps – swipe left or right with three fingers (swipe left or right with two fingers with the Magic Mouse)

- Swipe left from the right-hand edge of the trackpad or Magic Trackpad to access the Notification Center

- Access Mission Control (see page 87) – swipe up with three fingers (double-tap with two fingers with the Magic Mouse)

- App Exposé – swipe down with three fingers

- Access Launchpad – pinch with thumb and three fingers

- Show Desktop – spread with thumb and three fingers

Mission Control

Mission Control is a function in OS X Mavericks that helps you organize all of your open apps, full-screen apps and documents. It also enables you to quickly view the Dashboard and Desktop. Within Mission Control there are also Spaces, where you can group together similar types of documents. To use Mission Control:

1 Click on this button on the Dock, or

Click on a window in Mission Control to access it and exit the Mission Control window.

2 Swipe upwards with three fingers on the Magic Trackpad, or trackpad or double-tap with two fingers on a Magic Mouse

 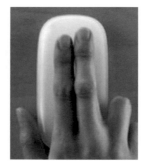

3 All open files and apps are visible via Mission Control

The top row of Mission Control contains the Dashboard, the Desktop and any full-screen apps.

...cont'd

4 If there is more than one window open for an app they will be grouped together by Mission Control

Beware

Any apps or files that have been minimized or closed do not appear within the main Mission Control window. Instead, they are located to the right of the dividing line on the Dock.

5 If an app is made full-screen it automatically appears along the top row

6 Desktop items are grouped together on the top row within Mission Control within an area called a Space (see pages 89-90)

Spaces and Exposé

The top level of Mission Control contains Spaces, which are areas into which you can group certain apps, e.g. the iLife apps such as iPhoto and iTunes. This means that you can access these apps independently from every other open item. This helps organize your apps and files. To use Spaces:

1 Move the cursor over the top right-hand corner of Mission Control

Preferences for Spaces and Exposé can be set within the Mission Control System Preference.

2 A new **Space** is created along the top row of Mission Control

Desktop 2

3 Drag an app onto the Space

Desktop 2

Hot tip

Create different Spaces for different types of content, e.g. one for productivity and one for entertainment.

4 Drag additional apps onto the Space

Desktop 2

...cont'd

When you create a new Space it can subsequently be deleted by moving the cursor over it and clicking on the cross at the left-hand corner. Any items that have been added to a Space that is then deleted are returned to the default Desktop Space.

5 When you create additional Spaces, the content of each Space is shown on its own when you access Mission Control

Exposé

Exposé is a function that enables you to view all of the open documents within an app. To use this:

If you are using a Magic Mouse, the Exposé function can be set with the F keys in the Mission Control System Preference. This is done within the Applications Windows option.

1 Position three fingers at the top of the Magic Trackpad, or trackpad, and swipe down

2 The open documents for the current app are displayed

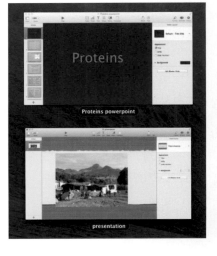

5 OS X Mavericks Apps

Apps, or applications, are the programs with which you start putting Mavericks to use, either for work or for fun. This chapter looks at using your apps and also the online App Store.

92 Launchpad

94 Full-Screen Apps

96 OS X Apps

97 Accessing the App Store

98 Downloading Apps

100 Finding Apps

102 Managing Your Apps

104 Sharing Apps

Launchpad

Even though the Dock can be used to store shortcuts to your applications, it is limited in terms of space. The full set of applications on your Mac can be found in the Finder (see Chapter Three) but OS X Mavericks has a feature that allows you to quickly access and manage all of your applications. These include the ones that are pre-installed on your Mac and also any that you install yourself or download from the Apple App Store. This feature is called Launchpad. To use it:

If the apps take up more than one screen, swipe from right to left with two fingers to view the additional pages. (For more information on Multi-Touch Gestures, see Chapter Four.)

92

To launch an app from within Launchpad, click on it once.

1 Click once on this button on the Dock

2 All of the apps (applications) are displayed

3 Similar types of apps can be grouped together in individual folders. By default, the **Utilities** are grouped in this way

4 To create a group of similar apps, drag the icon for one over another

5 The apps are grouped together in a folder and Launchpad gives it a name, based on the types of apps within the folder, usually the one into which the select app is placed

6 To change the name, click on it once and overtype it with the new name

7 The folder appears within the **Launchpad** window

8 To remove an app, click and hold on it until it starts to jiggle and a cross appears. Click on the cross to remove it

Full-Screen Apps

When working with apps we all like to be able to see as much of a window as possible. With OS X Mavericks this is possible with the full-screen app. This allows you to expand an app with this functionality so that it takes up the whole of your monitor or screen with a minimum of toolbars visible. Some apps have this functionality but some do not. To use full-screen apps:

1 By default an app appears on the desktop with other windows behind it

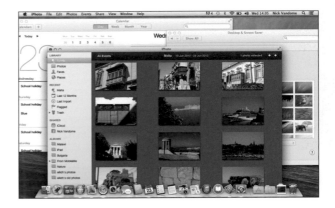

If the button in Step 2 is not visible then the app does not have the full-screen functionality.

2 Click on this button at the top right-hand corner of the app's window

3 The app is expanded to take up the whole window. The main Apple Menu bar and the Dock are hidden

4 To view the
main Menu bar,
move the cursor over the top of the screen

5 You can move between all full-screen apps by swiping
with three fingers left or right on a trackpad or Magic
Mouse

6 Move the cursor over the top right-hand corner
of the screen and click on this button to close
the full-screen functionality

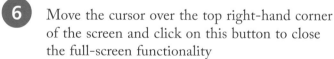

7 In Mission Control all of the open full-screen apps are
shown in the top row

Calendar   iPhoto   Safari

OS X Apps

OS X Mavericks apps include:

- **Automator**. An app for creating automated processes

- **Calculator.** A basic calculator

- **Calendar**. (See pages 110-111)

- **Chess**. Play online chess against your Mac computer

- **Contacts**. (See pages 108-109)

- **Dashboard**. (See page 106)

- **Dictionary**. A digital dictionary

- **DVD Player.** Used to play and view DVDs

- **FaceTime.** Can be used for video calls (See page 142)

- **Font Book.** Use this to add and change fonts

- **iBooks.** A new app for OS X Mavericks for downloading and buying books (See pages 152-153)

- **iPhoto, iTunes, iMovie, and GarageBand**. (See Chapter Eight)

- **Mail**. The default email app

- **Maps**. For viewing locations and destinations worldwide

- **Mission Control.** The function for organizing your desktop

- **Notes**. (See pages 112-113)

- **Photo Booth.** An app for creating photo effects

- **Preview.** (See page 122)

- **QuickTime Player**. The default application for viewing video

- **Reminders**. (See pages 114-115)

- **Safari**. The OS X specific Web browser

- **TextEdit**. An app for editing text files

- **Time Machine**. OS X's backup facility

Accessing the App Store

The App Store is another OS X app. This is an online facility where you can download and buy new apps. These cover a range of categories such as productivity, business and entertainment. When you select or buy an app from the App Store, it is downloaded automatically by Launchpad and appears there next to the rest of the apps.

To buy apps from the App Store you need to have an Apple ID account. If you have not already set this up, it can be done when you first access the App Store. To use the App Store:

The App Store is an online function so you will need an Internet connection with which to access it.

1 Click on this icon on the Dock or within the Launchpad

2 The Homepage of the App Store contains the current top featured apps

You can set up an Apple ID when you first set up your Mac or you can do it when you register for the App Store or the iTunes Store.

3 Your account information and quick link categories are listed at the right-hand side of the page

Downloading Apps

The App Store contains a wide range of apps: from small, fun apps, to powerful productivity ones. However, downloading them from the App Store is the same regardless of the type of app. The only differences are whether they require to be paid for or not and the length of time they take to download. To download an app from the App Store:

Hot tip

When downloading apps, start with a free one first so that you can get used to the process before you download paid-for apps.

98

1 Browse through the App Store until you find the required app

2 Click on the app to view a detailed description about it

3 Click on the button underneath the app icon to download it. If there is no charge for the app the button will say Free

4 If there is a charge for the app, the button will say **Buy App**

5 Click on the **Install App** button

6 Enter your **Apple ID** account details to continue downloading the app

Sign in to download from the App Store.
If you have an Apple ID, sign in with it here. If you have used the iTunes Store or iCloud, for example, you have an Apple ID. If you don't have an Apple ID, click Create Apple ID.

Apple ID
nickvandome@mac.com

Password
••••••••

Forgot?

Create Apple ID   Cancel   Sign In

Depending on their size, different apps take differing amounts of time to be downloaded.

7 The progress of the download is displayed in a progress bar underneath the Launchpad icon on the Dock

8 Once it has been downloaded, the app is available within Launchpad

Maps   iBooks

iMovie   Fotor

As you download more apps, additional pages will be created within the Launchpad to accommodate them.

Finding Apps

There are thousands of apps in the App Store and sometimes the hardest task is locating the ones you want. However, there are a number of ways in which finding apps is made as easy as possible:

1 Click on the **Featured** button

2 The main window has a range of categories such as New & Noteworthy and What's Hot. At the right-hand side there is a panel with the **Top Paid** apps

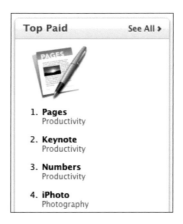

3 Underneath this is a list of the **Top Free** apps

4 Click on the **Top Charts** button

5 The top apps for different categories are displayed

6 Click on the **Categories** button

7 Browse through the apps by specific categories, such as Business, Entertainment and Finance

Managing Your Apps

Once you have bought apps from the App Store you can view details of ones you have purchased and also install updated versions of them.

Purchased Apps
To view your purchased apps:

1 Click on the **Purchases** button

2 Details of your purchased apps are displayed (including those that are free)

Even if you interrupt a download and turn off your Mac you will still be able to resume the download when you restart your computer.

3 If a download of an app has been interrupted, click on the **Resume** button to continue with it

Updating Apps

Improvements and fixes are being developed constantly and these can be downloaded to ensure that all of your apps are up-to-date:

1 When updates are available this is indicated by a red circle on the App Store icon in the Dock, in the same way as you would be alerted to new emails

2 Click on the **Updates** button

It is always worth updating your apps to improve them and download any security fixes as required.

3 Information about the update is displayed next to the app that is due to be updated

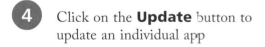

Earth 3D Lite
3Planesoft
Version 2.0.0
Released 19 November 2012

HUGE UPDATE!
• a redesigned landscape
• more detailed textures
• Retina support... ...More

4 Click on the **Update** button to update an individual app

UPDATE

5 Click on the **Update All** button to update all of the apps that are due to be updated

UPDATE ALL ▾

Apps can also be updated automatically. This can be specified in **System Preferences > App Store**. Check **On** the **Automatically check for updates** option. Underneath this there are options for downloading and installing updates.

Sharing Apps

If you have more than one Mac computer you do not have to buy apps separately for each one. If you have purchased an app for one Mac you can also install it on other Macs without having to pay for it again. To do this:

1 Access the App Store and click on the **Purchases** button

2 Any apps that have been purchased on another Mac are displayed in the Purchases window

Purchases		
OS X 10.9 Developer Preview Apple	11 June 2013
Pin for Pinterest FIPLAB Ltd	18 November 2012
iAntivirus Symantec	23 August 2012
Fun Photos Free Ohanaware Co., Ltd	21 August 2012
Two Towers FireBlink	17 August 2012
Cut the Rope ZeptoLab UK Limited	27 July 2012

To delete an app that has been downloaded, click and hold on it and drag it over the Trash icon on the Dock. Apps can also be deleted from the Launcher by holding down the Alt key and clicking the white cross on the app.

3 Click on the **Install** button to install an app on a Mac that does not yet have it

INSTALL

4 To install the app you will need to enter your Apple ID, although you will not be charged for the app

Sign in to download from the App Store.
If you have an Apple ID, sign in with it here. If you have used the iTunes Store or iCloud, for example, you have an Apple ID. If you don't have an Apple ID, click Create Apple ID.

Apple ID
nickvandome@mac.com

Password   Forgot?
••••••••

Create Apple ID   Cancel   Sign In

6 Getting Productive

There are several built-in apps within Mavericks that can be used to create, store and display information. This chapter shows how to access and use these apps, so that you can get the most out of Mavericks as a productive tool. These include apps for keeping organized and also maps for getting around.

106 Dashboard

107 Spotlight Search

108 Contacts (Address Book)

110 Calendar

112 Taking Notes

114 Setting Reminders

116 Notifications

118 Getting Around with Maps

122 Preview

123 Printing

124 OS X Utilities

126 Creating PDF Documents

Dashboard

The OS X Dashboard is a collection of widgets within OS X that can be used for common tasks such as a calendar, an address book and a dictionary. To use the Dashboard:

1 Click once on this icon on the Dock

2 The Dashboard widgets are maximized on the screen and superimposed over the rest of the active apps

106

3 Click here to view the panel of all of the available widgets (by default, only a selection is visible when the Dashboard is accessed)

4 The full range of widgets is shown here

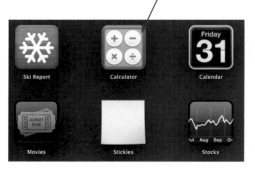

5 To make a widget active, drag it from the Dashboard panel onto the main window

Spotlight Search

Spotlight is the dedicated search app for OS X. It can be used over all the files on your Mac. To use Spotlight:

1 Click on this icon at the far right of the Apple Menu bar

2 In the Spotlight box, enter the search keyword(s)

Since the Spotlight search is always visible, it can be a quicker way to look for items than the Finder search.

3 The results are displayed according to type

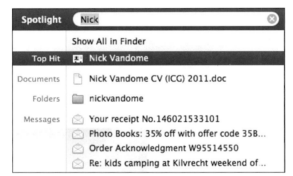

4 Click on an item to view it or see its contents

5 Options are also available for searching the Web or Wikipedia for the search keyword(s)

Spotlight starts searching for items as soon as you start typing a word. So don't worry if some of the first results look inappropriate as these will disappear once you have finished typing the full word.

6 Click on the **Spotlight Preferences...** link to specify the order, by category, in which results appear

Contacts (Address Book)

The Contacts app can be used to store contact information, which can then be used in different apps and shared via iCloud. To view and add contacts:

Hot tip

Contacts can be shared by clicking on the Share button and selecting one of the available options.

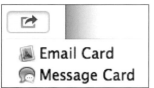

1 Open your **Contacts** and click on one in the left-hand panel to view their details

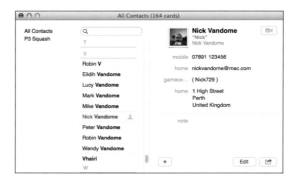

Adding contact information

The main function of the Contacts app is to include details of personal and business contacts. This has to be done manually for each entry, but it can prove to be a valuable resource once it has been completed. To add contact information:

Hot tip

Click on this button to add a new contact, rather than editing an existing one.

1 Click on the **Edit** button to edit contacts

2 Click on a category and enter contact information. Press the **Tab** key to move to the next field

3 Click on the **Done** button once you have edited the entry

Creating groups

In addition to creating individual entries in the Contacts app, group contacts can also be created. This is a way of grouping contacts with similar interests. Once a group has been created, all of the entries within it can be accessed and contacted by selecting the relevant entry in the left-hand panel. To create a group:

1 Select **File > New Group** from the menu bar to create a new group entry

2 Give the new group a name

3 Drag individual entries into the group (the individual entries are retained too)

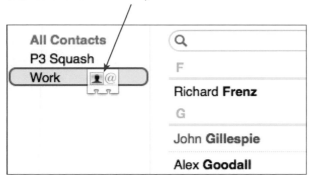

4 Click on a group name to view the members of the group

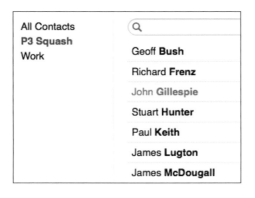

Individuals can be included in several groups. If you change their details in one group these changes will take effect across all of the groups in which the entry occurs.

Groups in your contacts can be used to send group emails, i.e. you can type the name of the group into the Mail To box to generate the names in the group and send the email to all of these recipients.

Hot tip

When Calendar is opened it displays the current date in the icon on the Dock.

Don't forget

Click on the **Today** button to view the current day. Click on the forward or back arrows to move to the next day, week, month or year, depending on what is selected in Step 2.

Calendar

Electronic calendars are now a standard part of modern life and with OS X this function is performed by the Calendar app. Not only can this be used on your Mac, it can also be synchronized with other Apple devices such as an iPod or an iPhone, using iCloud. To create a calendar:

1 Click on this icon on the Dock, or in the Launchpad

2 Select whether to view the calendar by day, week or month

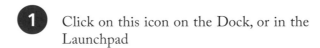

3 In month view, the current week is denoted by a light red line and the current day is denoted by a darker red band

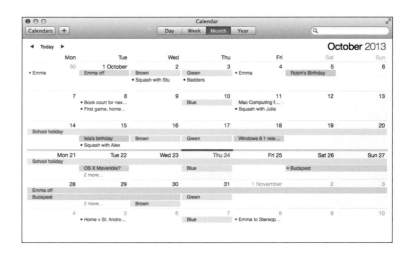

4 Scroll up and down to move through the weeks and months. In OS X Mavericks this is done with continuous scrolling which means you can view weeks across different months, rather than just viewing each month in its entirety, i.e. you can view the second half of one month and the first half of the next one in the same window

Adding Events

1 Select a date and double-click on it, or Ctrl + click on the date. Select **New Event**

2 Click on the **New Event** field and enter an event name

Click on this button to add a **Quick Event**, with just one text box for all of the relevant information. Once it has been added it can then be edited like a regular event by double-clicking on it.

3 Click on the date or time to amend it by entering new details. Check on the all-day box to set the event for a whole day

Finding Locations
When adding events you can also find details about locations:

1 Click on the **Add Location** field and start typing a destination. Suggestions will appear underneath, including matching items from your contacts list. Click on a location to select it

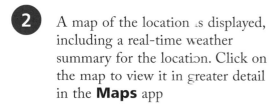

Other items that can be included for an event are: inviting people to it, calculating the travel time from your current location, creating a repeat event and setting an alert for it.

2 A map of the location is displayed, including a real-time weather summary for the location. Click on the map to view it in greater detail in the **Maps** app

Taking Notes

It is always useful to have a quick way of making notes of everyday things, such as shopping lists, recipes or packing lists for traveling. With Mavericks the Notes app is perfect for this task. To use it:

1 Click on this icon on the Dock, or in the Launchpad

2 The right-hand panel is where the note is created. The left-hand panel displays a list of all notes

The first line of a note becomes its heading in the left-hand panel.

112

3 Click on the note area and start typing to create a new note

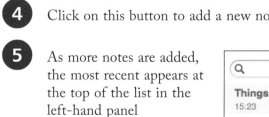

4 Click on this button to add a new note

5 As more notes are added, the most recent appears at the top of the list in the left-hand panel

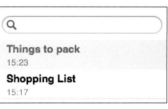

...cont'd

Sharing Notes

You can make your notes available on any other compatible devices that you have, through the use of iCloud. You can also share them with other people. To share your notes in these ways:

1 Click on the **Share** button at the bottom of a note to email the note or include it in an iMessage to someone

2 To makes notes available via iCloud, click on **Notes > Accounts...** from the Notes menu bar

3 Click on the **iCloud** button to access the iCloud System Preferences

4 Ensure that the box next to **Notes** is checked **On** in the iCloud System Preferences. Once this has been done, your notes will be available on other devices via iCloud

If you have an iCloud account, your notes can also be accessed by signing in to your account with your Apple ID at www.icloud.com

113

Setting Reminders

Another useful app for keeping organized is Reminders. This enables you to create lists for different topics and then set reminders for specific items. A date and time can be set for each reminder and, when this is reached, the reminder appears on your Mac screen (and in the Notification Center). To use Reminders:

Don't forget

As with Notes, iCloud makes your reminders available on all of your Apple devices, i.e. your Mac, iPad, iPhone and iPod Touch.

1 Click on this icon on the Dock, or in the Launchpad

2 Lists can be created for different categories of reminders. The Reminder lists are located in the left-hand panel. Click on a list name to add lists here

3 Click on these buttons to, from left to right, show or hide the lists panel, display a calendar for adding reminders on specific dates and adding a new list category

Hot tip

Roll over a reminder name to access the 'i' symbol for adding details to the reminder.

4 Click on this button to add a new reminder, or click on a new line

5 Enter text for the reminder

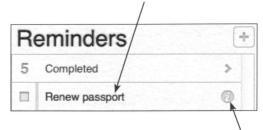

6 Click on this button to add details for the reminder

7 Check on this button to add a time and date for the reminder

8 Click on the date and select a date for when you want the reminder alert. Do the same for the time, by typing a new time over the one showing

For a recurring reminder, click on the Repeat link at Step 9 and select a repeat option from None, Every Day, Every Week, Every 2 Weeks, Every Month or Every Year.

9 If required, add details for a repeat reminder and a priority level

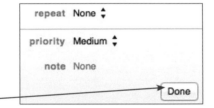

10 Click on the **Done** button

11 The reminder is set for the specified date and time. This will appear on the screen when the time arrives and also in Notifications, if it is set up for Reminders (see pages 116-117)

12 Check on this box to move a reminder to the Completed list

115

Notifications

The Notification Center option provides a single location to view all of your emails, messages, updates and alerts. It appears at the top right-hand corner of the screen. The items that appear in Notifications are set up within System Preferences. To do this:

Notifications can be accessed regardless of the app in which you are working, and they can be actioned directly without having to leave the current app.

Twitter and Facebook feeds can also be set up to appear in the Notification Center, if you have accounts with these sites.

1 Open System Preferences and click on this icon

2 The items that will appear in the Notification Center are listed here. Click on an item to select it and set its notification options

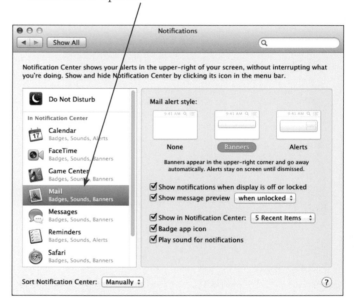

3 To disable an item so that it does not appear in the Notification Center, select it as above and check off the **Show in Notification Center** box

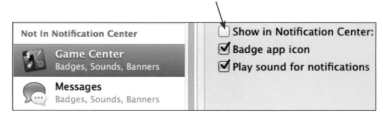

Viewing Notifications

Notifications appear in the Notification Center. The way they appear can be determined in the System Preferences:

1 Select an alert style. A banner alert comes up on the screen and then disappears after a few seconds

2 The **Alerts** option shows the notification and it stays on screen until dismissed (such as this one for reminders)

3 Click on this button in the top right-hand corner of the screen to view all of the items in the Notification Center. Click on it again to hide the Notification Center

4 In the Notification Center, click on an item to open it or view more details about it

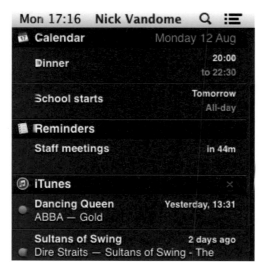

The Notification Center can also be displayed with a Trackpad or Magic Trackpad by dragging with two fingers from right to left, starting from the far right edge.

Software updates also appear in the Notification Center, when they are available.

117

Getting Around with Maps

With the Maps app you need never again wonder about where a location is, or worry about getting directions to somewhere. Using Maps with OS X Mavericks you will be able to do the following:

- Search maps around the world

- Find addresses

- Find famous buildings or landmarks

- Find the locations of the people in your Contacts app

- Get directions between different locations

- View traffic conditions

Viewing maps

Enable **Location Services** and then you can start looking around maps, from the viewpoint of your current location:

Location Services can be enabled in **System Preferences > Security & Privacy** and check on the **Enable Location Services** checkbox. Maps can be used without Location Services but this would mean that Maps cannot use your current location or determine anything in relation to this.

1 Click on this button on the Dock or in the Launcher

2 Click on this button to view your current location

3 Double-click to zoom in on a map. Alt + double-click to zoom out. Or, swipe outwards with thumb and forefinger to zoom in, and pinch inwards to zoom out

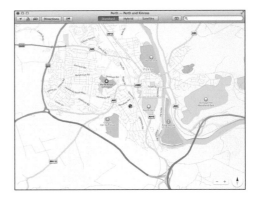

4 Or, click on these buttons to zoom in and out on a map

Finding locations

Locations in Maps can be found for addresses, cities or landmarks. To find items in Maps:

1 Enter an item into the Search box and click on one of the results

2 The selected item is displayed and shown on a map. Pins are also dropped at this point

3 Click on one of the buttons on the top Maps toolbar to view a **Standard**, **Hybrid** or **Satellite** view of the map

4 Click on the pin on the map to view its location

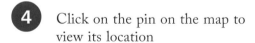

5 Click here to view more details about the location, including options for adding it as a contact and get directions to the location

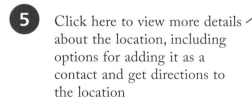

...cont'd

Getting directions

Within Maps you can also get directions to almost any location:

1 Click on the **Directions** button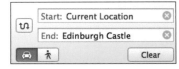

2 By default, your current direction is used for the **Start** field. If you want to change this, click once and enter a new location

3 Enter an **End** location or address

4 The route is shown on the map, with the directions down the right-hand side of the window. The default mode of transport is by car

5 Click on the **Share** button to send the directions to a mobile device, such as an iPhone or an iPad so that you can follow the directions on the go

Click on this button in Step 2 to swap the locations for which you want directions.

Click on this button in Step 2 to view the directions by foot instead of car.

Using Flyover

One of the innovative features in the Maps app is the Flyover function. This enables you to view locations, in 3D relief, as if you were moving over them from above. You can also zoom in and change the perspective. To use Flyover:

1 Access a map and select the **Satellite** option

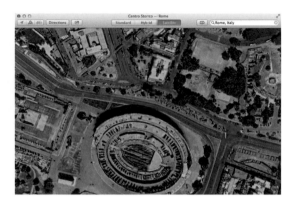

2 Click on this button to activate the Flyover functionality (if available for the area being viewed; if not it will be grayed-out)

3 The perspective changes so you are viewing the map from an angle. Click and drag on the map to move around it

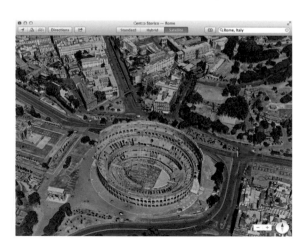

Hot tip

Swipe with two fingers on a trackpad to move around Flyover view. Swipe outwards with thumb and forefinger to zoom in and pinch inwards to zoom out again. Swivel with two fingers to change the viewing angle of the map.

Preview

Preview is an OS X app that can be used to view multiple file types, particularly image file formats. This can be useful if you just want to view documents without editing them in a dedicated app, such as an image editing app. Preview in OS X Mavericks can also be used to store and view documents in iCloud.

Don't forget

To open the Preview, click on this icon on the Dock or in the Launchpad.

Hot tip

Preview is also a good option for viewing PDF (Portable Document Format) documents.

Don't forget

Use these buttons in the Preview window to, from left to right, share selected items and add tags.

1 Open Preview and click on the **iCloud** button. (Click on the **On My Mac** button to open files from the Finder)

2 Drag files into the Preview window from the Finder to view them here and make them available in iCloud

3 Double-click on an item (from either the iCloud or On My Mac window) to view it at full size

122

Printing

OS X Mavericks makes the printing process as simple as possible, partly by being able to automatically install new printers as soon as they are connected to your Mac. However, it is also possible to install printers manually. To do this:

1 Open **System Preferences** and click on the **Printers & Scanners** button

2 Currently installed printers are displayed in the Printers List. Click here to add a new printer

3 Select an available printer

Name
Dell Laser Printer 1720dn

4 Click on the **Add** button to load the printer drivers for the selected printer

Add

5 The printer drivers are added

Setting up 'Dell Laser Printer 1720dn...'

Setting up the device...

Configure   Cancel

6 The printer is added in the **Printers & Scanners** window, ready for use

Don't forget

For most printers, OS X will detect them when they are first connected and they should be ready to use immediately without the need to install any software or apply new settings.

Don't forget

Once a printer has been installed, documents can be printed by selecting **File > Print** from the Menu bar. Print settings can be set at this point and they can also be set by selecting **File > Page/Print Setup** from the menu bar in most apps.

OS X Utilities

In addition to the apps in the Applications folder, there are also a number of utility apps that perform a variety of tasks within OS X. To access the Utilities:

Access the Launchpad to access the Utilities folder. The utilities are displayed within the Utilities folder

The Utilities folder is also available from within the Applications folder.

- **Activity Monitor**. This contains information about the system memory being used and disk activity (see page 180 for more details).

- **AirPort Utility**. This sets up the AirPort wireless networking facility.

- **AppleScript Editor**. This can be used to create your own scripts with Apple's dedicated scripting app, AppleScript.

- **Audio MIDI Setup**. This can be used for adding audio devices and setting their properties.

- **Bluetooth File Exchange**. This determines how files are exchanged between your computer and other Bluetooth devices (if this function is enabled).

- **Boot Camp Assistant**. This can be used to run Windows operating systems on your Mac.

- **ColorSync Utility**. This can be used to view and create color profiles on your computer. These can then be used by apps to try and match output color with monitor color.

- **Console**. This displays the behind-the-scenes messages that are being passed around the computer while its usual tasks are being performed.

- **DigitalColor Meter**. This can be used to measure the exact color values of a particular color.

You may never need to use a utility like the Console, but it is worth having a look at it just to see the inner workings of a computer.

- **Disk Utility**. This can be used to view information about attached disks and repair errors.

- **Grab**. This is a utility which can be used to capture screen shots. These are images of the screen at a given point in time. You can grab different portions of the screen and even menus. The resultant images can be saved into different file formats.

- **Grapher**. This is a utility for creating simple or more complex scientific graphs.

- **Java Preferences**. This is a folder that contains utilities that can be used to run and work with Java apps. It has specific utilities for Input Method Hotkey, Java Preferences and Java Web Start.

- **Keychain Access**. This deals with items such as passwords when they are needed for networking. These do not have to be set but it can save time if you have to enter passwords on a lot of occasions. It also ensures that there is greater security for items protected by passwords.

- **Migration Assistant**. This helps in the transfer of files between two Mac computers. This can be used if you buy a new Mac and you need to transfer files from another one.

- **Network Utility**. This is a problem determination guide to see if the problem is on the workstation or the network.

- **System Information**. This contains details of the hardware devices and software applications that are installed on your computer (see page 179 for more details).

- **Terminal**. This is used as an entry point into the world of UNIX. Within the Terminal you can view the workings of UNIX and also start to write your own apps, if you have some UNIX programming knowledge.

- **VoiceOver Utility**. This has various options for how the VoiceOver function works within OS X. This is the digital voice that can be used to read out what is on the screen and it is particularly useful for users who are visually impaired.

The Grab utility is useful if you are producing manuals or books and need to display examples of a screen or app.

The utilities are the workhorses of OS X. They do not have the glamor of apps such as iPhoto but they perform vital information gathering and general maintenance tasks.

Creating PDF Documents

PDF (Portable Document Format) is a file format that preserves the formatting of the original document and it can be viewed on a variety of computer platforms including Mac, Windows and UNIX. OS X has a built-in PDF function that can produce PDF files from most apps. To do this:

Don't forget

PDF files can be viewed with the Preview app.

1 Open a file in any app and select **File > Print** from the Menu bar. Click on the **PDF** button and click on **Save as PDF**

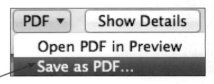

2 Browse to a destination for the file and click **Save**

Hot tip

PDF is an excellent option if you are creating documents such as instruction booklets, magazines or manuals.

3 Look in the selected location to view the newly created PDF file

7 Internet and Email

This chapter shows how to get the most out of the Internet and email. It covers connecting to the Internet and how to use the OS X web browser, Safari and its email app, Mail. It also covers Messages for text and photo messaging and FaceTime for video messaging and chatting.

128 Getting Connected

132 Safari

133 Safari Sidebar

134 Safari Tabbed Browsing

135 Safari Top Sites

136 Safari Reader

137 Adding Bookmarks

138 Mail

139 Using Email

140 Adding Mailboxes

141 Messaging

142 FaceTime

Getting Connected

Access to the Internet is an accepted part of the computing world and it is unusual for users not to want to do this. Not only does this provide a gateway to the World Wide Web but also email.

Connecting to the Internet with a Mac is done through the System Preferences. To do this:

1 Click on the **System Preferences** icon on the Dock

2 Click on the **Network** icon

3 Check that your method of connecting to the Internet is active, i.e. colored green

4 Click on the **Assist me...** button to access wizards for connecting to the Internet with your preferred method of connection

128

5 Click on the **Assistant...** button

Assistant...

6 The **Network Setup Assistant** is used to configure your system so that you can connect to the Internet

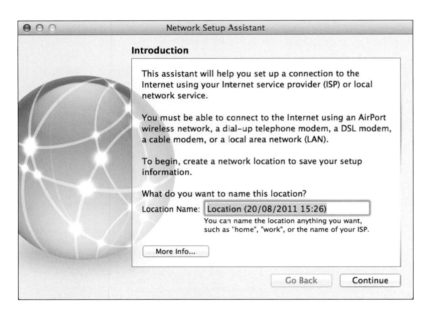

7 Enter a name for your connection

Location Name: My home

8 Click on the **Continue** button

Continue

...cont'd

9 Select an option for how you will connect to the Internet, e.g. wireless, cable or telephone modem

10 Click on the **Continue** button

Continue

11 For a wireless connection, select an available wireless network. This will be the router that is being used to make the connection

Select the wireless network you want to join:

CRAIGIE1

juicyanno

NETGEAR

12 Enter a password for the router (this will have been created when you connected and configured the router)

Password: Selected network requires a password

••••••••

13 Click on the **Continue** button

Continue

14 The **Ready to Connect** window informs you that you are about to attempt to connect to your network

15 Click on the **Continue** button

16 You are informed if the connection has been successful

17 Click on the **Done** button

Safari

Safari is a web browser that is designed specifically to be used with OS X. It is similar in most respects to other browsers, but it usually functions more quickly and works seamlessly with OS X.

Safari overview

1 Click here on the Dock to launch Safari

2 All of the controls are at the top of the browser

Toolbar Address/Search bar Reader Tabs

Favorites Bar and buttons Main content area

Smart Search box

One of the innovations in the latest version of Safari (7) is that the Address Bar and the Search Box have been incorporated into one item. You can use the same box for searching for an item or enter a web address to go to that page:

1 Click in the box to enter an item

Q Search Google or enter an address

2 Results are presented as web pages or search results. Click on the appropriate one to go to that item, i.e. directly to a website or to the search results page

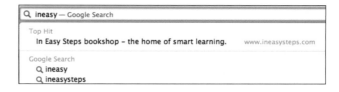

Q ineasy — Google Search

Top Hit
In Easy Steps bookshop - the home of smart learning.   www.ineasysteps.com

Google Search
Q ineasy
Q ineasysteps

Safari Sidebar

A new feature in Safari 7 on OS X Mavericks is the Safari Sidebar. This is a panel in which you can view all of your Bookmarks, Reading List items and Shared Links from social networking sites such as Twitter and LinkedIn

1 Select **View > Show Sidebar** from the Safari menu bar or click on this button

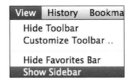

2 Click on the **Bookmarks** button to view all of the items that you have bookmarked. Click on the plus symbol **+** at the bottom of the Sidebar panel to add more folders for your bookmarks

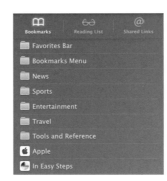

3 Click on the **Reading List** button to view all of the items that you have added to your reading list so that they can be read later, even if you are offline and not connected to the Internet. These can be added from the **Share** button

4 Click on the **Shared Links** button to view items that have been posted by your contacts on sites such as Twitter and LinkedIn

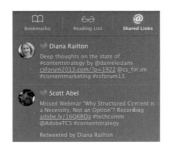

Links to social networking accounts can be set up in **System Preferences > Internet Accounts**. Select the required account and enter the details with which you log in to it. Updates will then be available in the Shared Links panel of the Sidebar.

Click on this button on the Safari toolbar to access web pages open on other Apple devices.

Safari Tabbed Browsing

Tabs are now a familiar feature on web browsers, so you can have multiple sites open within the same browser window:

Don't forget

Safari is a full-screen app and can be expanded by clicking the double arrow in the top right corner. For more information on full-screen apps, see pages 94-95.

1 When more than one tab is open, the tabs appear at the top of the web pages

2 Click on this button next to the tabs to open a new tab

3 Click on one of the **Top Sites** (see next page) or enter a website address in the Address Bar

4 Click on this button next to the New Tab button to minimize all of the current tabs

5 Move left and right to view all of the open tabs in thumbnail view. Click on one to view it at full size

Hot tip

Select **Safari > Preferences** from the Menu bar to specify settings for the way Safari operates.

Safari Top Sites

Within Safari there is a facility to view a graphical representation of the websites that you visit most frequently. This can be done from a button on the Safari Menu bar. To do this:

1 Click on this button to view the **Top Sites** window

The Top Sites window is also accessed if you open a new tab within Safari.

2 The Top Sites window contains thumbnails of the websites that you have visited most frequently with Safari (this builds up as you visit more sites)

3 Move the cursor over a thumbnail and click on the cross to delete a thumbnail from the **Top Sites** window. Click on the pin to keep it there permanently

Apple – OS X Mavericks – Do even mo...

Top Sites can also be added by opening the **Sidebar** and dragging a bookmarked site into the Top Sites window.

4 Click on a thumbnail to go to the full site

Safari Reader

Web pages can be complex and cluttered things at times. On occasions you may want to just read the content of one story on a web pages without all of the extra material in view. In Safari this can be done with the Reader function. To do this:

Beware

Not all web pages support the Reader functionality in Safari.

1 Select **View > Show Reader** from the Safari menu bar

Hot tip

Pages that are saved to a Reading List with the button in Step 6 can be read when you are offline, so you do not need to be connected to the Internet.

2 Click on the **Reader** button in the address bar of a web page that supports this functionality

3 The button turns a darker blue once the Reader is activated

4 The content is displayed in a text format, with a minimum of formatting from the original page

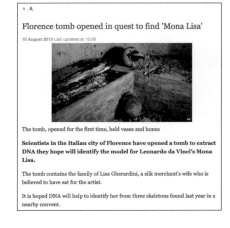

Don't forget

Other options can also be accessed from the **Share** button.

⌒⌐ Add to Reading List
📖 Add Bookmark
🖼 Email This Page
💬 Messages
🐦 Twitter
f Facebook

5 Click on the **Share** button on the Safari toolbar if you want to save a page to read later

6 Click on this button to add the page to your Reading List

Adding Bookmarks

Bookmarks is a feature by which you can create quick links to your favorite web pages or the ones you visit most frequently. Bookmarks can be added to a menu or the Bookmarks bar in Safari which makes them even quicker to access. Folders can also be created to store the less frequently used bookmarks. To view and create bookmarks:

1 Click here to view all bookmarks

2 All of the saved bookmarks can be accessed from the Sidebar

3 Click on the **Share** button and click on the **Add Bookmark** button to create a bookmark for the page currently being viewed, or press and hold on the **Add** button to the left of the Search/Address bar and select one of the options for where to add the page

Beware

Only keep your most frequently used bookmarks in the Bookmarks Bar, otherwise some of them will cease to be visible, as there will be too many entries for the available space.

4 Enter a name for the bookmark and select a location for it

5 Click on the **Add** button

Mail

Email is an essential element for most computer users and Macs come with their own email app called Mail. This covers all of the email functionality that anyone could need.

When first using Mail you have to set up your email account. This can be done with most email accounts and also a wide range of web mail accounts, including iCloud. To add email accounts:

Don't forget

Mail is a full-screen app and can be expanded by clicking the double arrow in the top right-hand corner. For more information on full-screen apps, see pages 94-95.

1 Click on this icon on the Dock

2 Check on the button next to the type of account that you want to create. If you have an Apple ID you will already have an iCloud email address which can be entered

3 Enter details of the account and click on the **Sign In** button

Don't forget

You can set up more than one account in the Mail app and you can download messages from all of the accounts that you set up.

4 Check on the **Mail** option for iCloud to sync your iCloud email across any other Apple devices and also the online account at **www.icloud.com**

Using Email

Mail enables you to send and receive emails and also format them to your own style. This can be simply formatting text or adding customized stationery. To use Mail:

1 Click on the **Get Mail** button to download available email messages

2 Click on the **New Message** button to create a new email

3 Click on the **Format** button to access options for formatting the text in the email

4 Click on these buttons to **Reply** to, **Reply** (to) **All** or **Forward** an email you have received

5 Select or open an email and click on the **Delete** button to remove it

6 Click on the **Junk** button to mark an email as junk or spam. This trains Mail to identify junk mail. After a period of time, these types of messages will automatically be moved straight into the Junk mailbox

7 Click on the **Attach** button to browse your folders to include another file in your email. This can be items such as photos, word documents or PDF files

8 Click on the **Show Stationery** button to access a variety of templated designs that can be added to your email

Hot tip

To show the text underneath an icon in Mail, Ctrl + click next to an icon and select **Icon & Text** from the menu.

Hot tip

When entering the name of a recipient for a message, Mail will display details of matching names from your Contacts. For instance, if you type DA, all of the entries in your Contacts beginning with this will be displayed and you can select the required one.

Hot tip

If you Forward an email with an attachment then the attachment is included. If you Reply to an email the attachment will not be included.

Adding Mailboxes

When you are dealing with email it is a good idea to create a folder structure (Mailboxes) for your messages. This will allow you to sort your emails into relevant subjects when you receive them, rather than having all of them sitting in your Inbox. To add a structure of new Mailboxes:

1 Click on this button to view your current Mailboxes

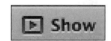

2 Click on the plus button at the bottom left-hand corner of the Mail window and select **New Mailbox**

3 Enter a name for the Mailbox and a location for where you would like it to be stored (by default this will be **On My Mac**)

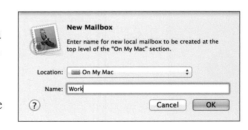

4 The new Mailbox is added to the current list

Messaging

The Messages app enables you to send text messages (iMessages) to other Mavericks users or those with an iPhone, iPad or iPod Touch using iOS 5 or above. It can also be used to send photos, videos and make FaceTime calls. To use Messages:

1 Click on this icon on the Dock

2 Click on this button to start a new conversation

3 Click on this button and select a contact (these will be from your Contacts app). To send an iMessage, the recipient must have an Apple ID

4 The person with whom you are having a conversation is displayed in the left-hand panel

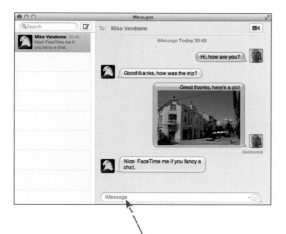

5 The conversation continues down the right-hand panel. Click here to write a message and press **Return** to send it. Drag photos or videos here to include them too

You require an Apple ID to use Messages and you will need to enter these details when you first access it. If you do not have an Apple ID you will be able to create one at this point.

141

To delete a conversation, roll over it in the left-hand panel and click on this cross.

FaceTime

FaceTime is an app that has previously been used on the iPhone and iPod touch to make video calls to other compatible devices. However, this is now available with OS X so that you can make and receive video calls from your Mac via iPhone, iPad and iPod Touch (with iOS 5 or later). To do this:

Don't forget

To use FaceTime you need to have an in-built FaceTime camera on your Mac or use a compatible external one.

142

1 Click on this icon on the Dock

2 You require an Apple ID to use FaceTime. Enter your details or click on the **Create New Account** button

Enter Apple ID

Sign in with your Apple ID or create a new account to activate FaceTime.

nickvandome@mac.com

••••••••

Sign In

Create New Account

Don't forget

If you receive a video call, you are alerted to this with a dialog box, even if FaceTime is not open and running.

3 Once you have logged in you can make video calls by selecting people from your address book, or adding their phone number, providing they have a device that supports FaceTime

8 Digital Lifestyle

Leisure time, and how we use it, is a significant issue for everyone. Within the OS X environment there are several apps that can be used to create and manage your digital lifestyle, including excellent options for photos, music and reading books.

144   iPhoto

145   Viewing Photos

146   Organizing Photos

147   Editing and Sharing Photos

148   iTunes

149   Managing Your Music

150   Purchasing Music

151   Adding an iPod

152   Reading with iBooks

154   Movies, Music and Games

iPhoto

iPhoto is the photo management app for OS X. The intention of iPhoto is to make the organizing, manipulation and sharing of digital images as easy as possible. To begin using iPhoto and downloading photos:

Don't forget

Once a camera has been connected to your Mac, iPhoto should open automatically.

1 Click once on this icon on the Dock

2 Connect your digital camera, or card reader, to your Mac via either USB or Firewire. The images on the connected device are displayed in the main iPhoto window

Hot tip

iPhoto is a full-screen app and when it is viewed in this mode the **Events**, **Photos**, **Faces** and **Places** buttons appear along the bottom of the screen rather than in the sidebar. To enter full-screen mode, select **View > Enter Full Screen** from the iPhoto menu bar.

3 Click on the **Import** button to import all of the images from the camera, or card reader

Import 641 Photos

4 Select specific images and click on the **Import Selected** button

Import Selected

Once photographs have been downloaded by iPhoto they are displayed within the Library. This is the main storage area for all of the photographs that are added to iPhoto.

Viewing Photos

There are a variety of ways in which photos can be viewed and displayed in iPhoto:

① Click on the **Events** button to view photos that are grouped by the date they were taken

② Drag the cursor through an Events thumbnail to scroll through the photos

③ Click on an Event to view the photos within it. Click on the **All Events** button to move back up one level

④ Double-click on a photo to view it at full size. Drag along the bottom thumbnail bar to view all of the photos within the event. Double-click on a full size photo to return to the thumbnails view

Hot tip

Click on the **Faces** button to view photos with people in them and tag the photos with individual names. Click on the **Places** button to view photos that have been tagged according to their location. To add a location to a photo, or an event, select it and click on the **Info** button on the bottom toolbar. Then keywords, face tagging and locations can be assigned to the photo. If you have a GPS-enabled camera then the location data will be stored when the photo is taken. Tagged photos are indicated by a red pin within the Places section. If a location cannot be assigned, open **iPhoto > Preferences > Advanced** and set **Look up Places** to **Automatically**.

Organizing Photos

Within iPhoto you can create albums to store different types of photos. To do this:

1 Select photos within the iPhoto window and click on the **Add To** button at the bottom right-corner of the main window

2 Click on the **Album** button

3 Click on the **New Album** button

4 Enter a name for the Album

5 The new album is included under the **Albums** section in the left-hand panel

6 To add photos to an album, drag them over the album name from the main iPhoto window

Once photos have been added to an album they are still visible in the main Library. The items in each album are just a reference back to the Library items.

Editing and Sharing Photos

As well as using iPhoto for viewing and organizing photos there are also facilities for editing and sharing them:

1 Click on this button to access the editing options

2 Click on the **Quick Fixes** tab for options to quickly edit various aspects of a photo, such as rotating it, color editing techniques and cropping

3 Click on the **Effects** tab to access various special effects that can be applied to a photo

4 Click on the **Adjust** tab to access a range of more sophisticated color editing options

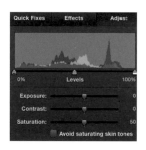

Most photos will benefit from some degree of editing but be careful not to overdo it, particularly with color editing and adjustments.

5 Click on the **Share** button to access options for sharing your photos to photo sharing sites and also popular social networking sites

iTunes

Music is one of the areas that has revived Apple's fortunes in recent years, primarily through the iPod music player and iTunes, and also the iTunes music store, where music can be bought online. iTunes is a versatile app but its basic function is to play a music CD. To do this:

1 Click on this button on the Dock and insert the CD in the CD/DVD drive

2 By default, iTunes will open and display this window. Click **No** if you just want to play the CD

Would you like to import the CD "100 Relaxing Classics [Disc 1]" into your iTunes library?

☐ Do not ask me again

No   Yes

Beware

Never import music and use it for commercial purposes as this would be a breach of copyright.

3 Click on the CD name in the Sidebar and double-click on a track to play it, or

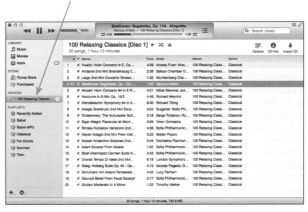

Hot tip

Notifications can be set to display each iTunes song as it begins to play. To do this, ensure **iTunes** is selected in **Notifications** within **System Preferences**.

4 Click on this button to play a track or a whole CD

5 Click on the **Import CD** button if you want to copy the music from the CD onto your hard drive

Import CD

Managing Your Music

iTunes has a variety of ways to display and manage your music:

1 Click on the **Music** button to see the iTunes categories, within a drop-down menu

2 Select **View > Show Sidebar** from the iTunes menu bar to display the left-hand sidebar. Click on the **Music** button to view all of your music content

3 Click on these buttons to view the details of your music according to these headings

4 Within any of the categories in Step 3, click on an item to view the songs within it. Double-click on a track to start playing it

5 When a song is playing it is displayed at the top of the iTunes window, along with controls to move to the next or previous track, pause and play the track and adjust the volume

Don't forget

iTunes can also be used to view movies, TV shows, podcasts and audiobooks that have been bought and downloaded from the **iTunes Store**.

Don't forget

Click on this button on the top toolbar when an album is playing to view all of the tracks that will play.

Purchasing Music

As well as copying music from CDs into iTunes, it is also possible to download a vast selection of music from the iTunes online store. To do this:

150

To buy music from the iTunes Store you must have an Apple ID and account.

1 Click on the **iTunes Store** link to access the online store

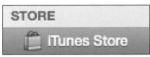

2 Navigate around the iTunes store using the tabs along the top of the iTunes window

3 To find a specific item, enter the details in the **Search** box at the top right-hand corner of the iTunes window

4 Details of the item are displayed within the Store. Click on the price button to buy and download the track or album

Adding an iPod

Since their introduction in 2001, iPods have become an inescapable part of modern life. It is impossible to sit on a bus or a train without seeing someone with the ubiquitous white earbuds, humming away to their favorite tunes. iPods are for everyone and they are designed to work seamlessly with iTunes and the latter can be used to load music onto the former. To do this:

1 Connect your iPod to the Mac with the supplied USB or Firewire cable

2 iTunes will open automatically and display details about the attached iPod

iPods come in a variety cf styles, colors, sizes and disk capacity.

3 iTunes should automatically start copying music from the iTunes Library onto the iPod. If not, select the **iPod** under the **Devices** heading

4 Select **File > Sync** from the iTunes Menu bar or click on the **Sync** button to synchronize iTunes and your iPod

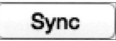

Reading with iBooks

iBooks is an eBook reading app that has been available with Apple's mobile devices, including the iPhone and the iPad, for a number of years. OS X Mavericks now brings this technology to desktop and laptop Macs. To use iBooks:

1 Click on this icon on the Dock or within the Launcher

iBooks consists of your own library for storing and reading eBooks and also access to the online iBooks Store for buying and downloading new books. Items that you have downloaded with iBooks on other devices will also be available in your iBooks Library on your Mac.

2 Click on the **Get Started** button

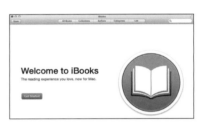

3 Click on the **Sign In** button to sign in with your Apple ID and access the iBooks Store. Click on the **Not Now** button to just access your iBooks Library

4 If you are signed in with your Apple ID, click on the **Go to the iBooks Store** button

Use these buttons on the top toolbar of the iBooks Store to view books by Featured, Top Charts and Top Authors.

5 The iBooks Store contains a wide range of books that can be previewed and downloaded

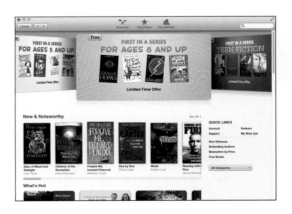

6 Click on a title to preview details about it

From the iBooks Store, click on the **Library** button in the top left-hand corner to go back to your own Library.

7 Click here to download the book (if it is a paid-for title this button will display a price)

8 The title will be downloaded into your iBooks Library. Double-click on the cover to open the book and start reading

Use these buttons on the top toolbar to, from left to right, go back to your Library, view the table of contents or view any notes you have added.

9 Click or tap on the right-hand and left-hand edges to turn a page. Move the cursor over the top of the page to access the top toolbar. The bottom toolbar displays the page numbers and location

Use these buttons on the top toolbar to, from left to right, change the page appearance, search for text and add a bookmark to a page.

Movies, Music and Games

With OS X Mavericks, your Mac really can become your own personal entertainment center. In addition to photos, music and books, there is also a range of apps that can be used to create your own movies, make music and play games. These can all be accessed in the **Applications** folder or from the **Launcher**.

iMovie

This is an app that can be used to create your own home movies. You can download footage from your video camera or smartphone and then edit it in iMovie. Numerous features can be added including transitions between scenes, text, music, voiceovers and special effects.

DVDs

In the past, Apple produced an app called iDVD for creating artistic presentations from your own home movies. However, this has now been discontinued, but other DVD-creation apps can be obtained in the App Store.

GarageBand

For anyone who wants to create their own music, this is the ideal app. There is a wide range of pre-set loops that can be used to build up music tracks and you can also select different instruments and create your own tracks by playing the onscreen keyboard which generates the music for the selected instrument.

Game Center

This app gives access (with an Apple ID) to an environment where you can not only play your favorite games and download more from the App Store, but also compare your scores and achievements against other Game Center players. It is also possible to compete directly against other people in multi-player games, where you can both play the same game simultaneously.

Other apps from creating movies and music can also be downloaded from the App Store.

9 Sharing OS X

This chapter looks at how to set up different user accounts and how to keep everyone safe on your Mac using parental controls.

156 Adding Users

158 Deleting Users

159 Fast User Switching

160 OS X for the Family

161 Parental Controls

164 OS X for Windows Users

Adding Users

OS X enables multiple users to access individual accounts on the same computer. If there are multiple users, i.e. two or more, for a single machine, each person can sign on individually and access their own files and folders. This means that each person can log in to their own settings and preferences. All user accounts can be password protected, to ensure that each user's environment is secure. To set up multiple user accounts:

Don't forget

Every computer with multiple users has at least one main user, also known as an administrator. This means that they have greater control over the number of items that they can edit and alter. If there is only one user on a computer, they automatically take on the role of the administrator. Administrators have a particularly important role to play when computers are networked together. Each computer can potentially have several administrators.

1 Click on the **System Preferences** icon on the Dock

2 Click on the **Users & Groups** icon

3 The information about the current account is displayed. This is your own account and the information is based on details you provided when you first set up your Mac

Don't forget

Each user can select their own icon or photo of themselves.

4 Click on this icon to enable new accounts to be added (the padlock needs to be open)

Click the lock to prevent further changes.

5 Click on the plus sign icon to add a new account

6 Enter the details for the new account holder

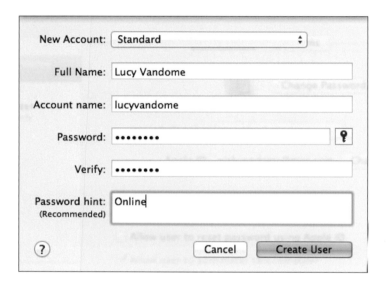

By default, you are the administrator of your own Mac. This means that you can administer other user accounts.

7 Click on the **Create User** button

Create User

8 The new account is added to the list in the Accounts window, under **Other Users**

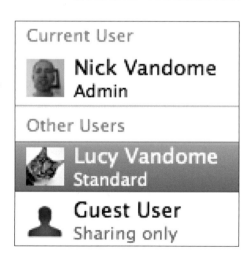

Deleting Users

Once a user has been added, their name appears on the list in the Accounts preference dialog box. It is then possible to edit the details of a particular user or delete them altogether. To do this:

Beware

Always tell other users if you are planning to delete them from the system. Don't just remove them and then let them find out the next time they try to log in. If you delete a user, their personal files are left untouched and can still be accessed.

158

1 Within **Users & Groups**, select a user from the list

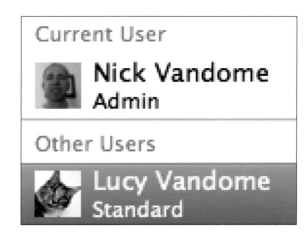

2 Click here to remove the selected person's user account

3 A warning box appears to check if you really do want to delete the selected user. If you do, select the required option and click on **OK**

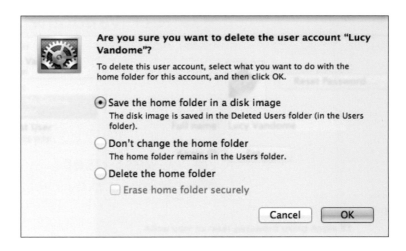

Fast User Switching

If there are multiple users using OS X it is useful to be able to switch between them as quickly as possible. When this is done, the first user's session is retained so that they can return to it if required. To switch between users:

1 In the Users & Groups window, click on the **Login Options** button

2 Check on the **Show fast user switching menu** box

☑ Show fast user switching menu as [Full Name ⬍]

3 At the top-right of the screen, click on the current user's name

4 Click on the name of another user

Don't forget

When you switch between users, the first user remains logged in and their current session is retained intact.

5 Enter the relevant password (if required)

6 Click on this button to log in

OS X for the Family

Many families share their computers between multiple users and with the ability to create different accounts in OS X, each user can have their own customized workspace. If desired, you can also set up an Apple ID so that other users can access a wider range of products, such as the Apple App Store. To do this:

1 Access **Users & Groups**

Users & Groups

2 Click on the **Apple ID Set...** button

3 If the user already has an Apple ID, enter it in the appropriate box. If not click on the **Create Apple ID** button to create an account

4 A page on the Apple website is accessed. This contains general information about an Apple ID and also a facility for obtaining one

Parental Controls

If children are using the computer parents may want to restrict access to certain types of information that can be viewed, using Parental Controls. To do this:

1 Access **Users & Groups** and click on a username. Check on the **Enable Parental Controls** box and click on the **Open Parental Controls...** button

2 Click on the **Apps** tab

3 Check on the **Use Simple Finder** box to show a simplified version of the Finder

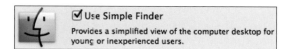

4 Check on this box if you want to limit the types of app that a user can access

5 Check off the boxes next to the apps that you do not want used

6 Click here to select options for age limits in terms of accessing items in the App Store

Hot tip

To check which sites have been viewed on a web browser, check the History menu, which is located on the main Menu bar.

161

...cont'd

Web controls

1 Click on the **Web** tab

2 Check on this button to try to prevent access to websites with adult content

3 Check on this button to specify specific websites that are suitable to be viewed

People controls

1 Click on the **People** tab

2 Check on the **Limit** boxes to limit the type of content in the Game Center, email messages and iMessages

...cont'd

Time Limits controls

1 Click on the **Time Limits** tab

Time Limits

2 Check on this box to limit the amount of time the user can use the Mac during weekdays

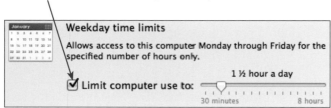

3 Check on this box to limit the amount of time the user can use the Mac during weekends

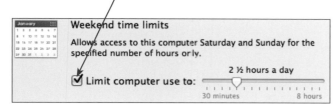

4 Check on these boxes to determine the times at which the user cannot access their account

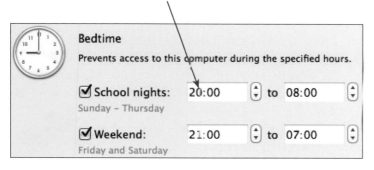

OS X for Windows Users

General sharing

One of the historical complaints about Macs is that it is difficult to share files between them and Microsoft Windows computers. While this may have been true with some file types in years gone by, this is an issue that is becoming less and less important, particularly with OS X. Some of the reasons for this are:

- A number of popular file formats, such as PDFs (Portable Document Format) for documents and JPEGs (Joint Photographic Experts Group) for photos and images, are designed so that they can be used on both Mac and Windows platforms.

- A lot of software apps on the Mac have options for saving files into different formats, including ones that are specifically for Windows machines.

- Other popular apps, such as Microsoft Office, now have Mac versions and the resulting files can be shared on both formats.

Sharing with Boot Camp

For people who find it hard to live without Microsoft Windows, help is at hand even on a Mac. Macs have an app called Boot Camp that can be used to run a version of Windows on a Mac. This is available with Mavericks. Once it has been accessed, a copy of Windows can then be installed and run. This means that if you have a non-Mac app that you want to use on your Mac, you can do so with Boot Camp.

Boot Camp is set up with the Boot Camp Assistant which is located within the Utilities folder within the Applications folder. Once this is run you can then install either Windows XP, Vista, Windows 7, Windows 8, or Windows 8.1, which will run at its native speed. The Boot Camp Assistant utility installs support software for Windows, creates a partition on your hard drive for it and starts the Windows Installer. There is also a Help page link that provides detailed instructions about installing Windows on your Mac.

Hot tip

A lot of file formats can be opened on both Macs and Windows PCs. Even Word, Excel and PowerPoint files can be exchanged, as long as each user has the relevant version of Office.

10 Networking

This chapter looks at networking and how to share files over a network.

166 Networking Overview

168 Network Settings

169 File Sharing

170 Connecting to a Network

Networking Overview

Before you start sharing files directly between computers, you have to connect them together. This is known as networking and can be done with two computers in the same room, or with thousands of computers in a major corporation. If you are setting up your own small network it will be known in the computing world as a Local Area Network (LAN). When setting up a network there are various pieces of hardware that are initially required to join all of the required items together. Once this has been done, software settings can be applied for the networked items. Some of the items of hardware that may be required include:

- **A network card.** This is known as a Network Interface Card (NIC) and all recent Macs have them built-in.

- **An Ethernet port and Ethernet cable.** This enables you to make the physical connection between devices. Ethernet cables come in a variety of forms but the one you should be looking for is the Cat5E type as this allows for the fastest transfer of data. If you are creating a wireless network then you will not require these.

- **A hub.** This is a piece of hardware with multiple Ethernet ports that enables you to connect all of your devices together and let them communicate with each other. However, conflicts can occur with hubs if two devices try to send data through it at the same time.

- **A switch.** This is similar in operation to a hub but it is more sophisticated in its method of data transfer, thus allowing all of the machines on the network to communicate simultaneously, unlike a hub.

- **A wireless router.** This is for a wireless network which is increasingly the most common way to create a network. The router is connected to a telephone line and the computer then communicates with it wirelessly.

Once you have worked out all of the devices that you want to include on your network, you can arrange them accordingly. Try to keep the switches and hub within relative proximity of a power supply and, if you are using cables, make sure they are laid out safely.

Hot tip

If you have two Macs to be networked and they are in close proximity then this can be achieved with an Ethernet crossover cable. If you have more than two computers, then this is where an Ethernet hub is required. In either case, there is no need to connect to the Internet to achieve the network.

Ethernet network

The cheapest and easiest way to network computers is to create an Ethernet network. This involves buying an Ethernet hub or switch, which enables you to connect several devices to a central point, i.e. the hub or switch. All Apple computers and most modern printers have an Ethernet connection, so it is possible to connect various devices, not just computers. Once all of the devices have been connected by Ethernet cables, you can then start applying network settings.

AirPort network

Another option for creating a network is using Apple's own wireless system, AirPort. This creates a wireless network and there are two main options used by Apple computers: AirPort Express, using the IEEE 802.11n standard, which is more commonly known as Wi-Fi, which stands for Wireless Fidelity, and the newer AirPort Extreme, using the next generation IEEE 802.11ac standard which is up to five times faster than the 802.11n standard. Thankfully, AirPort Express and Extreme are also compatible with devices based on the older IEEE standards, 802.11b/g/n, so one machine loaded with AirPort Extreme can still communicate wirelessly with an older AirPort one.

One of the issues with a wireless network is security, since it is possible for someone with a wireless-enabled machine to access your wireless network if they are within range. However, in the majority of cases the chances of this happening are fairly slim, although it is an issue about which you should be aware.

The basics of a wireless network with Macs is an AirPort card (either AirPort Express or AirPort Extreme) installed in all of the required machines and an AirPort base station that can be located anywhere within 150 meters of the AirPort enabled computers. Once the hardware is in place, wireless-enabled devices can be configured by using the AirPort Setup Assistant utility found in the Utilities folder. After AirPort has been set up, the wireless network can be connected. All of the wireless-enabled devices should then be able to communicate with each other, without the use of a multitude of cables.

Wireless network

A wireless network can also be created with a standard wireless router, rather than using the Aiport option.

Don't forget

Another method for connecting items wirelessly is called Bluetooth. This covers much shorter distances than AirPort and is usually used for items such as printers and smartphones. Bluetooth devices can be connected by using the Bluetooth Setup Assistant in the Utilities folder.

Network Settings

Once you have connected the hardware required for a network, you can start applying the network settings that are required for different computers to communicate with one another. To do this (the following example is for networking two Mac computers):

1 In **System Preferences**, click on the **Network** button

2 For a wireless connection, click on the **Turn Wi-Fi On** button

3 Details of wireless settings are displayed

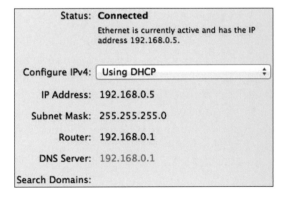

4 For a cable connection, connect an **Ethernet** cable

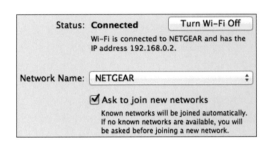

5 Details of the cable settings are displayed

Status: **Connected**
Ethernet is currently active and has the IP address 192.168.0.5.

Configure IPv4: Using DHCP

IP Address: 192.168.0.5

Subnet Mask: 255.255.255.0

Router: 192.168.0.1

DNS Server: 192.168.0.1

Search Domains:

6 Click on the **Advanced...** button to see the full settings for each option

File Sharing

One of the main reasons for creating a network of two or more computers is to share files between them. On networked Macs, this involves setting them up so that they can share files and then accessing these files.

Setting up file sharing

To set up file sharing on a networked Mac:

1 Click on the **System Preferences** button on the Dock

2 Click on the **Sharing** icon

3 Check on the boxes next to the items you want to share (the most common items to share are files and printers)

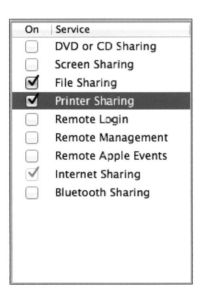

4 Click on the padlock to close it and prevent more changes

Hot tip

For OS X Mavericks users, files can also be shared with the AirDrop option. This can be used with two Macs that have this facility. When it s accessed, files can be shared simply by dragging them onto the icon of the other user that appears in the AirDrop window. To access AirDrop, click on this button in the Finder window.

169

Beware

If no file sharing options are enabled in the **Sharing** preference window, no other users will be able to access your computer or your files, even on a network.

Connecting to a Network

Connecting as a registered user

To connect as a registered user (usually as yourself when you want to access items on another one of your own computers):

1 Other connected computers on the network will show up in the Shared section in the Finder. Click on a networked computer

2 Click on the **Connect As...** button

3 Check on the **Registered User** button and enter your username and password

4 Click on the **Connect** button

5 The public folders and home folder of the networked computer are available to the registered user. Double-click on an item to view its contents

Don't forget

You can disconnect from a networked computer by ejecting it in the Finder in the same way as you would for a removable drive such as a DVD.

170

...cont'd

Guest users

Guest users on a network are users other than yourself, or other registered users, to whom you want to limit access to your files and folders. Guests only have access to a folder called the Drop Box in your own Public folder. To share files with Guest users you have to first copy them into the Drop Box. To do this:

1 Create a file and select **File > Save** from the Menu bar

2 Navigate to your own home folder (this is created automatically by OS X and displayed in the Finder Sidebar)

If another user is having problems accessing the files in your Drop Box, check the permissions settings that have been assigned to the files. See page 186 for further details.

3 Double-click on the **Public** folder

4 Double-click on the **Drop Box** folder

The contents of the Drop Box can be accessed by other users on the same computer as well as users on a network.

5 Save the file into the Drop Box

...cont'd

Accessing a Drop Box

To access files in a Drop Box:

Beware

It is better to copy files into the Drop Box rather than moving them completely from their current location.

1 Double-click on a networked computer in the Finder

2 Click on the **Connect As...** button in the Finder window

3 Check on the **Guest** button

Connect as: ● Guest
○ Registered User

4 Click on the **Connect** button

Connect

5 Double-click on a user's **Public** folder

Hot tip

Set permissions for how the Drop Box operates by selecting it in the Finder and Ctrl + clicking on it. Select **Get Info** from the menu and apply the required settings under the **Ownership & Permissions** heading.

Nick Vandome's Public Folder

6 Double-click on the **Drop Box** folder to access the files within it

Drop Box

SHARED
iMac

(11) Maintaining OS X

Despite its stability, OS X still benefits from a robust maintenance regime. This chapter looks at ways to keep OS X in top shape, ensure downloaded apps are as secure as possible and some general troubleshooting.

174 Time Machine

178 Disk Utility

179 System Information

180 Activity Monitor

181 Updating Software

182 Gatekeeper

183 Privacy

184 Problems with Apps

185 General Troubleshooting

Time Machine

Time Machine is a feature of OS X that gives you great peace of mind. In conjunction with an external hard drive, it creates a backup of your whole system, including folders, files, apps and even the OS X operating system itself.

Once it has been set up, Time Machine takes a backup every hour and you can then go into Time Machine to restore any files that have been deleted or become corrupt.

Setting up Time Machine

To use Time Machine it has to first be set up. This involves attaching a hard drive to your Mac. To set up Time Machine:

Make sure that you have an external hard drive that is larger than the contents of your Mac. Otherwise Time Machine will not be able to back it all up.

1 Click on the **Time Machine** icon on the Dock or access it in the System Preferences

2 You will be prompted to set up Time Machine

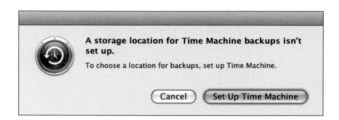

3 Click on the **Set Up Time Machine** button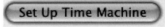

4 In the Time Machine System Preferences window, click on the **Select Disk...** button

5 Connect an external hard drive and select it

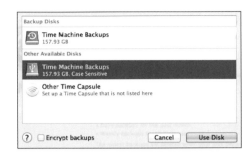

6 Click on the **Use for Backup** button

7 In the Time Machine System Preferences window, drag the button to the **On** position

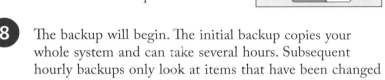

8 The backup will begin. The initial backup copies your whole system and can take several hours. Subsequent hourly backups only look at items that have been changed since the previous backup

9 The progress of the backup is displayed in the System Preferences window and also here

Beware

When you first set up Time Machine it copies everything on your Mac. Depending on the type of connection you have for your external drive, this could take several hours, or even days. Because of this it is a good idea to have a hard drive with a Firewire connection to make it as fast as possible.

Don't forget

If you stop the initial backup before it has been completed, Time Machine will remember where it has stopped and resume the backup from this point.

175

...cont'd

Using Time Machine

Once the Time Machine has been set up it can then be used to go back in time to view items in an earlier state. To do this:

Beware

If you have deleted items before the initial set up of Time Machine, these will not be recoverable.

1 Access an item on your Mac and delete it. In this example image **DSC_0134** has been deleted

2 Click on the **Time Machine** icon

3 The Time Machine displays the current item in its current state (the image is deleted). Earlier versions are stacked behind it

Don't forget

The active item that you were viewing before you launch Time Machine is the one that is active in the Time Machine interface. You can select items from within the active window to view their contents.

4 Click on the arrows to move through the open items or select a time or date from the scale to the right of the arrows

5 Another way to move through the Time Machine is to click on the pages behind the front one. This brings the selected item to the front. In this example, Time Machine has gone back to a date when the image was still in place, i.e. before it was deleted

Items are restored from the Time Machine backup disk, i.e. the external hard drive.

6 Click on the **Restore** button to restore the item that has been deleted

7 Click on the **Cancel** button to return to your normal environment

8 The deleted image **DSC_0134** is now restored in its original location

Disk Utility

Disk Utility is a utility app that allows you to perform certain testing and repair functions for OS X. It incorporates a variety of functions and it is a good option for general maintenance and if your computer is not running as it should.

Each of the functions within Disk Utility can be applied to specific drives and volumes. However, it is not possible to use the OS X start-up disk within Disk Utility as this will be in operation to run the app and Disk Utility cannot operate on a disk that has apps already running. To use Disk Utility:

Checking disks

1 Click the **First Aid** tab to check a disk

2 Select a disk and select one of the first aid options

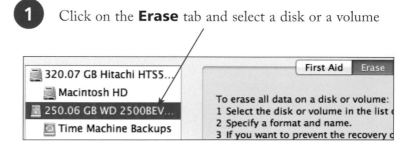

Erasing a disk
To erase all of the data on a disk or a volume:

1 Click on the **Erase** tab and select a disk or a volume

2 Click **Erase** to erase the data on the selected disk or volume

Disk Utility is located within the **Applications > Utilities** folder.

If there is a problem with a disk and OS X can fix it, the **Repair** button will be available. Click on this to enable Disk Utility to repair the problem.

If you erase data from a removable disk, such as a pen drive, you will not be able to retrieve it.

System Information

This can be used to view how the different hardware and software elements on your Mac are performing. To do this:

1 Open the **Utilities** folder and double-click on the **System Information** icon

2 Click on the **Hardware** link and click on an item of hardware

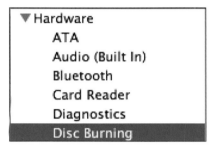

▼ Hardware
ATA
Audio (Built In)
Bluetooth
Card Reader
Diagnostics
Disc Burning

System Information is located within the **Applications > Utilities** folder.

3 Details about the item of hardware, and its performance, are displayed

```
MATSHITA DVD-R  UJ-898:

Firmware Revision:  HE13
Interconnect:       ATAPI
Burn Support:       Yes (Apple Shipping Drive)
Cache:              1024 KB
Reads DVD:          Yes
CD-Write:           -R, -RW
DVD-Write:          -R, -R DL, -RW, +R, +R DL, +RW
Write Strategies:   CD-TAO, CD-SAO, DVD-DAO
Media:              To show the available burn speeds, insert a disc
                    and choose View > Refresh
```

4 Click on software items to view their details

```
Calendar                                6.0
Canon IJ Printer Utility              7.27.0

Calendar:

Version:        6.0
Last Modified:  23/06/2012 08:26
Kind:           Intel
64-Bit (Intel): Yes
App Store:      No
Location:       /Applications/Calendar.app
```

Activity Monitor

Activity Monitor is a utility app that can be used to view information about how much processing power and memory is being used to run apps. This can be useful to know if certain apps are running slowly or crashing frequently. To use Activity Monitor:

Activity Monitor is located within the **Applications > Utilities** folder.

Activity Monitor

1 Click on the **CPU** tab to see how much processor capacity is being used up

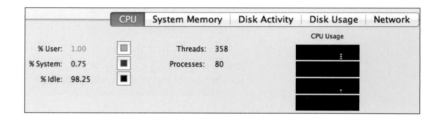

2 Click on the **System Memory** tab to see how much system memory (RAM) is being used up

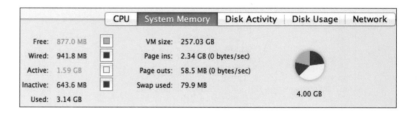

3 Click on the **Disk Usage** tab to see how much space has been taken up on the hard drive

Updating Software

Apple periodically releases updates for its software; both its apps and the OS X operating system. All of these are now available through the App Store. To update software:

1 Open **System Preferences** and click on the **App Store** icon

2 Click here to select options for how you are notified about updates and how they are downloaded

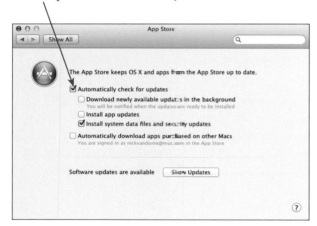

3 If updates are available, click on the **Show Updates** button

4 Available updates are shown in the Updates section in the App Store. Click on the **Update** buttons to update

If automatic updates is selected, you will be alerted at the appropriate time when updates are available. This is done through the Notification Center.

Check on the Automatically download apps purchased on other Macs box if you want to activate this function.

For some software updates, such as those to OS X itself, you may have to restart your computer for them to take effect.

Gatekeeper

Internet security is an important issue for every computer user; no-one wants their computer to be infected with a virus or malicious software. Historically, Macs have been less prone to attack from viruses than Windows-based machines, but this does not mean Mac users can be complacent. With their increasing popularity there is now more temptation for virus writers to target them. Mavericks recognizes this and has taken steps to prevent attacks with the Gatekeeper function. To use this:

Hot tip

To make changes within the General section of the Security & Privacy System Preferences, click on the padlock icon and enter your admin password.

1 Open **System Preferences** and click on the **Security & Privacy** button

Security & Privacy

2 Click on the **General** tab  General

3 Click on these buttons to determine which apps can be downloaded. You can select from just the Mac App Store, or Mac App Store and identified developers, which gives you added security in terms of apps having been thoroughly checked

Don't forget

Apple have a very robust checking procedure for apps in the App Store and those produced by identified developers.

Allow apps downloaded from:

○ Mac App Store
◉ Mac App Store and identified developers
○ Anywhere

4 Under the **General** tab there are also options for using a password when you log in to your account and also if a password is required after sleep or the screen saver

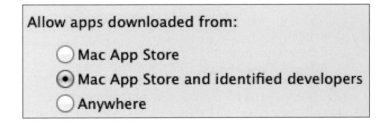

A login password has been set for this user [Change Password...]

☑ Require password [immediately ⬍] after sleep or screen saver begins
☐ Show a message when the screen is locked [Set Lock Message...]
☐ Disable automatic login

Privacy

Also within the Security & Privacy System Preferences are options for activating a firewall and privacy settings:

1 Click on the **Firewall** tab

2 Click on the **Turn On Firewall** button to activate this

3 Click on the **Privacy** tab

4 Click on the **Location Services** link and check On the **Enable Location Services** if you want relevant apps to be able to access your location

5 Click on the **Contacts** link and check On any relevant apps that want to access your Contacts

6 Click on the **Diagnostics & Usage** link and check On the **Send diagnostic & usage data to Apple** if you want to send information to Apple about the performance of your Mac and its apps. This will include any problems and helps Apple improve its software and apps. This information is collected anonymously and does not identify anyone personally

Mavericks apps are designed to do only what they are supposed to, so that they do not have to interact with other apps if they do not need to. This lessens the possibility of any viruses spreading across your Mac. For instance, only apps that can use Contacts will ask for permission to do this.

Problems with Apps

The simple answer

OS X is something of a rarity in the world of computing software: it claims to be remarkably stable, and it is. However, this is not to say that things do not sometimes go wrong, although this is considerably less frequent than with older Mac operating systems. Sometimes this will be due to problems within particular apps and on occasions the problems may lie with OS X itself. If this does happen, the first course of action is to close down OS X using the **Apple menu > Shut Down** command. Then restart the computer. If this does not work, or you cannot access the Shut Down command, try turning off the power to the computer and then starting up again.

Force quitting

If a particular app is not responding it can be closed down separately without the need to reboot the computer. To do this:

1 Select **Apple menu > Force Quit** from the Menu bar

2 Select the app you want to close

3 Click **Force Quit**

General Troubleshooting

It is true that things do go wrong with OS X, although probably with less regularity than with some other operating systems. If something does go wrong, there are a number of items that you can check and also some steps you can take to ensure that you do not lose any important data if the worst case scenario occurs and your hard drive packs up completely:

- **Backup**. If everything does go wrong it is essential to take preventative action in the form of making sure that all of your data is backed up and saved. This can be done with either the Time Machine app or by backing up manually by copying data to a CD or DVD.

- **Reboot**. One traditional reply by IT helpdesks is to reboot, i.e. turn off the computer and turn it back on again and hope that the problem has resolved itself. In a lot of cases this simple operation does the trick but it is not always a viable solution for major problems.

- **Check cables**. If the problem appears to be with a network connection or an externally connected device, check that all cables are connected properly and have not worked loose. If possible, make sure that all cables are tucked away so that they cannot be inadvertently pulled out.

- **Check network settings**. If your network or Internet connections are not working, check the network setting in System Preferences. Sometimes when you make a change to one item this can have an adverse effect on one of these settings. (If possible, lock the settings once you have applied them, by clicking on the padlock icon in the Network preferences window.)

- **Check for viruses**. If your computer is infected with a virus this could affect the efficient running of the machine. Luckily this is less of a problem for Macs as virus writers tend to concentrate their efforts towards Windows-based machines. However, there are plenty of Mac viruses out there, so make sure your computer is protected by an app such as Norton AntiVirus which is available from **www.symantec.com**

In extreme cases, you will not be able to reboot your computer normally. If this happens, you will have to pull out the power cable and re-attach it. You will then be able to reboot, although the computer may want to check its hard drive to make sure that everything is in working order.

...cont'd

● **Check Start-up items**. If you have set certain items to start automatically when your computer is turned on, this could cause certain conflicts within your machine. If this is the case, disable the items from launching during the booting up of the computer. This can be done within the Accounts preference of System Preferences by clicking on the **Startup Items** tab, selecting the relevant item and pressing the minus button.

● **Check permissions**. If you, or other users, are having problems opening items this could be because of the permissions that are set. To check these, select the item in the Finder, click on the **File** button on the Finder toolbar and select **Get Info**. In the **Ownership & Permissions** section of the Info window you will be able to set the relevant permissions to allow other users, or yourself, to read, write or have no access.

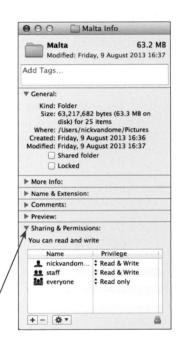

Click here to view permissions settings

● **Eject external devices**. Sometimes external devices, such as pen drives, can become temperamental and refuse to eject the disks within them, or even show up on the desktop or in the Finder. If this happens you can eject the disk by pressing the mouse button when the Mac chimes are heard during the booting up process.

● **Turn off your screen saver**. Screen savers can sometimes cause conflicts within your computer, particularly if they have been downloaded from an unreliable source. If this happens, change the screen saver within the **Desktop & Screen Saver** preference of the System Preferences or disable it altogether.

A

About Your Mac	12-15
Display information	14
Memory information	16
Overview	13
Storage information	15
Accessibility	21-22
Activity Monitor	124, 180
Address book.	See Contacts
AirDrop	169
AirPort	167
AirPort Utility	124
Apple ID	39, 97, 141, 150, 160
Apple menu	10
AppleScript Editor	124
Apps	
Automator	96
Calculator	96
Calendar	96
Chess	96
Contacts	96
Dashboard	96
Deleting	104
Dictionary	96
Downloading	98-99
DVD Player	96
FaceTime	96
Finding	100-101
Font Book	96
GarageBand	96
iBooks	96
iMovie	96
iPhoto	96
iTunes	96
Mail	96
Managing	102-103
Maps	96
Mission Control	96
Notes	96
OS X apps	96
Photo Booth	96
Preview	96
Purchased	102
QuickTime Player	96
Reminders	96
Safari	96
Searching for	100
Sharing	104
TextEdit	96
Time Machine	96
Updating	103
Automatically	103
App Store	97
Accessing	97
Categories	101
Featured	100
Top Charts	101
Top Free	100
Top Paid	100
Using with an Apple ID	97
Aqua interface	11
Audio MIDI Setup	124
Automator	96

B

Background	
Changing	18
Bluetooth File Exchange	124
Books.	See iBooks
Boot Camp	164
Boot Camp Assistant	124, 164

C

Calendar	110-111
Adding Events	111
Continuous scrolling	110
Finding locations	111
Chess	96
Color adjustments.	
See iPhoto: Editing and sharing photos	
ColorSync	124
Console	124
Contacts	108
Contact information	
Adding	108
Groups	
Creating	109
Copy and paste	57
Copying	
By dragging	57
Covers	52

D

Dashboard	106
Making widgets active	106
Overview	106
Desktop	10, 42
Showing	81
Desktop items	42
Dictation	23
Dictionary	96
DigitalColor Meter	124
Disk Utility	125, 178
Checking disks	178
Erasing a disk	178
Dock	
Adding items	33
Genie effect	29
Keep in Dock option	33
Magnification	29
Menus	32
Overview	26
Positioning	28
Preferences	28-30
Quit option	32
Removing items	34
Removing open apps	34
Resizing manually	29
Show In Finder option	32
Stacking items	30-31
Drop Box	
Accessing	172
DVDs	
Creating	154

E

eBooks.	See iBooks
Effects.	See iPhoto: Editing and sharing photos
Ejecting items	43
Email	
Mailboxes	
Adding	140
Using	139-140
Enhancing photos.	
	See iPhoto: Editing and sharing photos
Ethernet	166
Excel	164
Exposé	89-90
External devices	
Ejecting	186

F

Facebook	37
FaceTime	142
Family.	See OS X: For the family
Fast user switching	159
Finder	46-56
Actions button	46, 68
All My Files	47
Applications	48
Arrangement button	69
Back button	49
Documents	48
Folders	47-48
Home folder	48
Overview	46
Search	56
Sharing from	69
Sidebar	55
Adding items to	55
Tabs	60-61
Tags	62-63, 68
Toolbar	
Customizing	54
Views	49-54
Column view	51
Icon view	50-51
List view	51-52
Finding things	
Using Finder	56
Flickr	69
Flyover.	See Maps: Using Flyover
Folders	
Burnable	65
Creating new	58
Spring-loaded	64
Force quitting	184
Full-Screen Apps	94

G

Game Center	154
Games	
Playing	154
GarageBand	96, 154
Gatekeeper	182
Google	56
Grab	125
Grapher	125

I

iBooks	152-153
Library	153
Previewing titles	153
Toolbars for books	153
iCloud	38-41
Keychain	41
Online account	40
Setting up	39
Storage	38
Using	40
iDVD	
Discontinued	154
iMessages	141
iMovie	96, 154
Internet	
Getting connected	128-131
Internet Accounts	
Adding	133
Internet Service Provider	128
iOS 5 or above	
For messaging	141
iPhoto	96, 144-147
Adjust	147
Editing and sharing photos	147
Effects	147
Importing images	144
Organizing photos	146
Quick Fixes	147
Share	147
Viewing photos	145
iPod	148
Adding	151
iTunes	96, 148-150
Managing music	149
Purchasing music	150
iTunes Store	150

J

Java Preferences	125
JPEG	154

K

Keychain Access	125
Keynote	41

L

Labeling items	68
LAN	166
Launchpad	92-93
LinkedIn	37

M

Magic Mouse	72
Gestures	82-84
Magic Trackpad	72
Mail	96, 138-140
Overview	138
Maps	96, 118-121
Finding locations	119
Getting directions	120
Hybrid	119
Satellite	119
Standard	119
Using Flyover	121
Viewing	118
Menus	11, 70
Main menu bar	
Apple menu	70
Edit menu	70
File menu	70
Finder menu	70
Go	70
Help	70
View	70
Window	70
Messages	141
Microsoft Office	164
Microsoft Windows	
Sharing with	164
Migration Assistant	125
Mission Control	87-88, 96
Mountain Lion	
About	8
Movies	
Creating	154
Moving between full-screen apps	80
Moving between pages	80
Multiple displays	36
Multiple users	
Adding users	156-157
Multi-Touch Gestures	86
Multi-Touch Preferences	85-86
More Gestures	86

Point & Click   86
Scroll & Zoom   86
Music
    Creating   154
    Importing   148

N

Navigating   72
Network
    File sharing
        Drop Box   172
        Guest users   172
        Setting up   169
Networking
    AirPort base station   167
    AirPort Express   167
    Airport Extreme   167
    Airport network   167
    Connecting to a network   170-171
    Ethernet cable   166
    Ethernet network   167
    File sharing   169-172
    Hub   166
    IEEE 802.11 standards   167
    Network card   166
    Network settings   168
    Overview   166-167
    Router
        Wireless   166
    Switch   166
    Wi-Fi   167
    Wireless network   167
Network Interface Card   166
Network Utility   125
Notes   112-113
Notification Center   116-117
Notifications   116-117
    Alerts   117
    Viewing   117
Numbers   41

O

Option buttons   11
Organizing music.   See iTunes: Managing music
OS X
    For the family   160
    For Windows users   164

OS X Mavericks
    About   8
    Compatible Mac computers   9
    From the App Store   9
    Installing   9
    Working environment   10
OS X Utilities   124-125

P

Pages   41
Parental controls   161-163
    Enable   161
    People controls   162
    Time Limits controls   163
    Web controls   162
PDF   164
    Creating documents   126
Playing music.   See iTunes
Powerpoint   164
Preview   122
Printing   123
Privacy   183
Programs (apps)
    Problems   184
        Force quitting   184

Q

Quartz   11
Quick Look   53

R

RAM   180
Reading List   136
Reminders   114-115
Removable disks   42
Resolution
    Changing   20
    Screen   20
Resuming   24, 44

S

Safari   96, 132-137
  Bookmarks
    Adding   137
  Overview   132
  Reader   136
  Share button   136
  Shared Links   133
  Sidebar   133
  Tabbed browsing   134
  Top Sites   135
Screen burn   19
Screen readers   22
Screen saver
  Changing   19
Scroll bars   73
Scrolling
  Up and down   76-77
Searching   56
Selecting
  By clicking   66-67
  By dragging   66
  Select All   67
Sharing
  For Windows users   164
  From the Finder   69
Sharing photos. *See* iPhoto: Editing and sharing photos
Shutting down   24
Social networking
  Linking to accounts   37
Social networking accounts
  Adding   133
Social networks
  Sharing photos with   147
Software updates   117, 181
Spaces   89-90
  Deleting   90
Spotlight   56, 107
  Preferences   107
  Search   107
System Information   179
System Preferences   36-37
  About   17
  Hardware   36
    CDs & DVDs   36
    Displays   36
    Energy Saver   36
    Keyboard   36
    Mouse   36
    Printers & Scanners   37
    Sound   37
    Trackpad   36
  Internet & Wireless   37
    Bluetooth   37
    iCloud   37
    Internet Accounts   37
    Network   37
    Sharing   37
  Personal   36
    Desktop & Screen Saver   36
    Dock   36
    General   36
    Language & Region   36
    Mission Control   36
    Notifications   36
    Security & Privacy   36
    Spotlight   36
  System   37
    Accessibility   37
    App Store   37
    Date & Time   37
    Dictation & Speech   37
    Parental Controls   37
    Startup Disk   37
    Time Machine   37
    Users & Groups   37
System Information   125

T

Tabbed browsing   134
Tabs.   *See* Finder: Tabs
Tags.   *See* Finder: Tags
Terminal   125
TextEdit   96
Text to Speech   23
Time Machine   96, 174-177
  Setting up   174
  Using   176
Trackpad   72
Trash   35
  For deleting apps   104
Troubleshooting
  Backing up   185
  Cables   185
  External devices   186
  Network settings   185
  Overview   185
  Permissions   186
  Rebooting   185
  Screen savers   186
  Start-up items   186
  Viruses   185
Twitter   37, 69

U

UNIX	8
User accounts	
Deleting users	158
Fast user switching	159
Utilities	
Activity Monitor	124
AirPort Utility	124
AppleScript Editor	124
Audio MIDI Setup	124
Bluetooth File Exchange	124
Boot Camp Assistant	124
ColorSysc Utility	124
Console	124
DigitalColor Meter	124
Disk Utility	125
Grab	125
Grapher	125
Java Preferences	125
Keychain Access	125
Migration Assistant	125
Network Utility	125
System Information	125
Terminal	125
VoiceOver Utility	125

V

Viewing files	
Without opening	53
Viewing photos.	See iPhoto: Viewing photos
VoiceOver	21
VoiceOver Utility	125

W

Window buttons	11
Windows	
7	164
8	164
8.1	164
Vista	164
XP	164
Wireless network.	See Networking
Word	164
World Wide Web	128

Z

Zooming in and out	
With gestures	78-79